EXTRAVAGANT PRAISE

Our History, Heritage, and Hope

Andi Oney

Ordering Information: Quantity sales. Special discounts are available on quantity purchases by corporations, associations, and others. For details, please see our website: AndiOney.com.

Printed in the United States of America.
First Printing, 2016
www.AndiOney.com

ISBN-13: 978-1541088481
ISBN-10: 1541088484

DEDICATION

Lovingly dedicated to Larry,
a sign of God's love for me
and reason to give God praise.

Feast of the Immaculate Conception
December 8, 2016

CONTENTS

Dear Reader,

When I first met Andi Oney many years ago, I was attracted to her beauty and her beautiful demeanor. I thought that she displayed that "hidden person of the heart with the imperishable jewel of a gentle and quiet spirit which in God's sight is very precious" (I Pet. 3:4). I knew her to be a woman with a deep love for her husband, family and the people of God and a woman who loved and studied the Word of God.

My husband Al and I were with Andi in that Upper Room in Jerusalem when the Glory of God was manifest and Al was the one who placed his hand on her head and told her that the Lord was releasing her into ministry in a new way. That prophetic word has been fulfilled in a marvelous fashion. The Lord has chosen for that "hidden person of the heart" to be more widely known. It has been a joy to see how the Lord is anointing and using Andi to proclaim the Gospel and to lead people into the Baptism in the Spirit ever since that outpouring in the Cenacle. The Spirit of the Lord is raising her up as a bright light to be His instrument to the nations.

I have been both blessed and challenged by Andi's teaching in Extravagant Praise. She lives what she proclaims here about total surrender to Jesus and the call to live for the praise of His glory. I've been with her as she and her husband lead others into exuberant praise in tongues and in the festal shout. I've witnessed the way the power of God comes down when she ministers. As you read this book, you will also be encouraged and challenged to deepen your intimacy with Jesus Christ, to open yourself to the baptism in the Spirit and to grow in a life of praise.

May you discover the beauty of this soul, Andi Oney, who in union with Our Lady, is proclaiming the greatness of the Lord and whose spirit is rejoicing in God her Savior. Indeed, God who is mighty has done great things for her and holy is His Name! (Cf. Luke 1:46-49)

Patti Mansfield
As By A New Pentecost: Golden Jubilee Edition
Leader in the Catholic Charismatic Renewal

Dear Reader,

It is with great pleasure and gratitude that I recommend, in the highest terms, the new book, *Extravagant Praise: Our History, Heritage, and Hope* by Andi Oney. This is not only a book about prayer, but an invitation to the reader to pray. Andi displays a wealth of knowledge about the Scriptures and those texts which have guided the Church at prayer through the ages. Her style of writing is engaging without being intrusive; challenging without being judgmental; and inviting while respecting the reader's freedom. Andi's emphasis on praise serves as an important reminder that we are most authentically human when we acknowledge our dependency on the God in whom we live, move, and have our being.

This recognition of our dependency moves our spirit to praise in gratitude to the God who gives good gifts to those who ask. I invite all who wish to begin a life of prayer, as well as those who are looking for a deeper relationship with the Lord, to read and pray Andi's much needed book. You will be deeply enriched through the Holy Spirit. As you read, meditate, and pray the message on these pages, your being will be prayerfully lifted to the God through whom we are wonderfully made. Andi's new book is a most valuable gift to those who desire to praise the Lord.

Rev. William F. Maestri
Archdiocese of New Orleans

Preface
An Invitation to Praise

When Saint Pope John Paul II took his apostolic journey to the United States and Canada in 1987, I was a privileged pilgrim witnessing the Holy Father, who had such love for young people. I was a teenager attending the gathering in the Louisiana Superdome on September 12, 1987, along with other members of our church youth group. At the time, I had no idea of what a profound gift, instrument of holiness, and wealth of catechesis our dear Holy Father was to the Church. On this occasion, I was honoring the Vicar of Christ on earth, a holy and faithful apostle, a man desiring oneness with God who won the affection of many. It was years later that I would come to fully appreciate this profound opportunity to be in the presence of a saint in the making.

The message of the Holy Father to the young people gathered in New Orleans included two major themes:

mission and prayer. He encouraged young people not to be deceived, but to follow the truth, the person of truth, Jesus Christ. He spoke about individual responsibilities and interdependence upon one another. On this day, we heard and experienced the truth delivered by a descendant of the apostles, our spiritual father on earth.

> Each of us is *an individual*, a person a creature of God, one of his children, someone very special whom God loves and for whom Christ died. This identity of ours determines the way we must live, the way we must act, the way we must view our mission in the world. We come from God, we depend on God. *God has a plan for us* – a plan for our lives, for our bodies, for our souls, for our future. This plan for us is extremely important – so important that God became man to explain it to us.[1]

The message is timeless and one that could have been recorded and played over and over for each generation even to the present. The second part of his message is given in the same spirit of pastoral and fatherly love, and speaks to people of all ages. His comments are really an encouraging catechesis on prayer that begins with praise. His instruction was to look to Jesus Himself as our model of prayer. It is evident in the personhood of Saint Pope John Paul II, that he himself modeled this formula for prayer as he truly exemplified joy.

> First of all, we know that his prayer is marked by a spirit of joy and praise. "*Jesus rejoiced in the Holy Spirit* and said: "I offer you praise, O Father, Lord of heaven and earth" (Ibid. 10, 21). In addition, he entrusted to the Church at the Last Supper the celebration of the Eucharist, which remains for all ages the most perfect means of offering to the Father glory and thanksgiving and praise.[2]

It is fitting that the Holy Father mentions not only praise and joy, but the ultimate celebration of praise, the Eucharist. These words given to young people are in direct contradiction to the narcissism that often pervades society. Being faithful to prayer is one thing, but to first honor God and give Him praise in a spirit of joy puts our hearts in focus: off of self and looking to God. This is an act of humility.

The Holy Father's approach to encourage young people to pray was both balanced and realistic. He mentions the times of suffering, pain, and struggle which are part of any young person's journey. Again, he encouraged us to look to Jesus who, "poured out his heart to God, seeking to find in his Father both comfort and support."[3] He specifically mentions the prayer of Jesus in the Garden of Gethsemane and reminds us how "*in his anguish he prayed with all the greater intensity*."[4] He said when struggles and temptations come, "We must do the same!"[5]

As any good teacher, the Holy Father mentions the importance of not giving up our efforts, especially in prayer. He challenges us to "*turn to the Bible* and to *the Church's liturgy*."[6] As I have come to learn myself, the Psalms are the prayers of the people of God and are an account of salvation history, complete with rejoicing, lamenting, repentance, prophecy, and victory. The Holy Father encourages, "try to make your own the beautiful prayer of the Psalms. You will find in the inspired word of God the spiritual food you need. Above all your soul will be refreshed when you take part wholeheartedly with the community in the celebration of the Eucharist, the church's greatest prayer."[7]

As we will examine later, the celebration of the Eucharist includes many forms of prayer, but mostly the prayer of praise. His brief catechesis on prayer continues as he brings up the subject of prayers that are most readily on the lips of the faithful: petition.

> When you pray, you must realize that prayer is not just asking God for something or seeking special help, even though prayers of petition are true ways of praying. But prayer

> should also be characterized by *thanksgiving and praise*, by *adoration and attentive listening* by *asking God's pardon* and forgiveness."[8]

As a young person attending this Apostolic gathering, I don't think those words really took root in my heart. The prayers of thanksgiving and praise were practiced, but not with great intention. I was participating in acts of praise and thanksgiving, such as the mass, but I can say that my heart had not fully accepted the responsibility to simply praise God with no agenda. In learning more about the powerful act of praise, I see it as the preparation prayer that sets the stage for all other prayers that follow. Praise can put things in new perspectives, right and better perspectives, and free us to whole-heartedly seek his will and meaning in the situations of life. This is the ultimate goal of prayer—to honor God first; and second, to participate in his divine will for us.

In his closing remarks, I am reminded again today of the continual action of the Holy Spirit in our lives. The Holy Father took us back to joy, a fruit of the Holy Spirit. "It is significant that the symbol of the Holy Spirit on Pentecost was tongues of fire. In fact, fire is often the symbol that the Bible uses to speak of the action of God in our lives. For the Holy Spirit truly inflames our hearts, engendering in the enthusiasm for the works of God. And when we pray, the Holy Spirit stirs up within us love of God and love of our neighbour."[9] It's the Holy Spirit who will remind us of our responsibility to pray, and likewise teach us to praise. The Holy Father's final words, "The Holy Spirit brings us joy and peace...... These are the gifts which only the Holy Spirit can give."[10]

Since that blessed occasion, I have grown to know a brilliant and beloved Apostle in Saint Pope John Paul II. His treasure of teachings, apostolic exhortations, letters, and catechesis have been life changing to many Christians around the world. His witness of forgiveness, devotion to Our Lady, attention to the Holy Spirit, his compassion and message of mercy, and his holy and dignified last days have marked Christianity with a taste of divinity touching humanity. When I reread his remarks from 1987 in New Orleans, I was excited to hear again his message in support of giving praise to God. I consider it no accident that the unction to praise God that wells up in me were seeds planted by Saint Pope John Paul II. Now that's reason to praise!

Fast-forward about 25 years. It's November 2013 and I find myself not just in Jerusalem, but in the Upper Room. This is the sacred space where Jesus instituted the

Eucharist. This is the place where Jesus went after being raised from the dead, showed Himself to the disciples, and breathed peace upon them. In this room, where the apostles and Mary, the Mother of Jesus and others numbering about 120, gathered to wait as Jesus instructed for the promise of the Father. This sacred space, where the promise of the Father—the Holy Spirit—came in a dramatic way. In this room, I found myself part of a chorus of praise going up to God the Father like incense before Him. It was spontaneous yet reverent praise. It was communal yet personal praise. I was a voice crying out to God and sensing in my heart that I was participating in my own personal Pentecost.

I believe praise is the gift that sustains our personal Pentecost. Praise is the bridge linking our heritage of praise to our heavenly praise. This Upper Room experience fulfilled the message of Saint Pope John Paul II that I had heard so many years earlier. Praise like Jesus in a spirit of joy with intensity and allow the Holy Spirit to enflame your heart and teach you to praise. On Pentecost, the Holy Spirit broke in upon a group huddled in prayer in the Upper Room and transformed the lives of those encountering Him. I consider it grace that it happened that way for me.

Chapter 1
Foundations of Praise

There are a few truths about praise that we must consider in order to better appreciate its meaning and depth. I consider these truths the four pillars of praise. Each function individually, but at the same time, build upon each other to give us a better understanding of praise:

I. "Praise is a form of prayer." (CCC 2639) In order to have a relationship with the One True God, we have to live a life of prayer.

II. "Prayer is the raising of one's mind and heart to God or the requesting of good things from God." (CCC 2559)

III. "Humility is the foundation of prayer." (CCC 2559)

IV. "The Holy Spirit whose anointing permeates our whole being, is the

> interior Master of Christian prayer." (CCC 2672)

There are many ways to describe the word "praise," both secular and spiritual. The secular or worldly definitions would not exist but for the origin of praise associated with the things of God who created both. My exploration and experience of the prayer of praise is like a newfound discovery titled, *Getting Back to Basics.* I believe praise is the original prayer of every heart. There is great power in genuine praise. This power is not something to acquire or achieve, but rather something to receive, experience, and express.

As with all prayer, praise requires humility. Humility is the virtue most associated with offering any type of prayer to God because, when we pray, we put ourselves under his Lordship. When we humble ourselves and give praise to God, we also put ourselves in a position to receive the grace that God offers when our hearts sing out to honor Him.

The secular acts of praising others for good works are on the rise. We live in a culture that focuses so much on itself that society gives huge accolades to people who are doing what any Christian living for the Kingdom should do. In a time when we have 24 hour "news" much of this is media driven. In my attempt to present praise as a prayer superiorly intended for God, it is not my goal to diminish honoring others for extraordinary works for God or mankind. As a former teacher, I have experienced the benefits and results of praising a student both for acceptable behavior and for applied thinking strategies. The benefits of praise in the workplace are likewise effective, often verbal but mostly represented monetarily. Mankind flourishes when we are acknowledged for the good that we do, but offering praise to God is something altogether different.

Much of my life as a Christian was lived in ignorance about the truth of praise that was due God. Praise is a fundamental concept, but I really hadn't considered it a real "prayer." My prayer of praise went as far as being thankful for the things God had provided me. It is beautiful and beneficial when we have a heart of gratitude for all that God has done. However, there is so much more to praise than being thankful. What separates our praise to God from all other praise is that we praise Him for who He is—period. Unlike a person holding a distinguished political office, the clergy, our parents or grandparents, or any other person whom we see as honorable, God is above all. We can honor or respect those who hold positions even if we don't always agree with them. In fact, most of us do honor the "position" above the person. We can honor or respect the person even if we have personal differences simply because of their role. To praise God is to praise the One who created everything in the universe; He who is above all things and knows all things. St. Paul, a man filled with the Holy Spirit and who knew how to praise God, addresses the Ephesians with his message of unity. In it he refers to the Lord as "one God and Father of all, who is over all and through all and in all." (Ephesians 4:6). He who created us uniquely for Himself, God, who holds the supreme office – Creator.

The Catechism of the Catholic Church gives us further insight into the prayer of praise. It states that praise "is the form of prayer which recognizes most immediately that God is God. It lauds God for his own sake and gives him glory, quite beyond what he does, but simply because HE IS. It shares in the blessed happiness of the pure of heart who love God in faith before seeing him in glory." (CCC 2639). When you or I see someone who we know, we recognize them for who they are. In fact, we don't recognize people we don't know. There is a difference between knowing someone and knowing of someone. I had someone once tell me, "I don't know this God you profess to know. I go to church, I am devoted to prayer, but I don't see Him move in my life." My response: praise. I immediately began to praise because praise recognizes God for who He is, not for what He's done or didn't do. I encourage those with this sense of longing to know God or to know Him more intimately or for the grace to recognize His movement in your life to continue to praise Him as an act of obedience. The Scripture tells us to enter His gates with thanksgiving in our hearts, and to enter His courts with praise. (see Psalm 100:4) A prayer of praise should always be first when we seek the Lord.

Even in difficulty or dry seasons our praise can create an avenue to come to truly know Him and not simply know of Him. As the popular interpretation of Psalm 22 given to us by the King James Bible says, God inhabits the praise of his people. (Psalm 22:3) God so desires for us to know Him. Any heart crying out to God to know Him more intimately, He will not refuse. I believe that Satan would like to have us believe the lie that it's difficult to really know God. It would be unfair for God to make our relationship so difficult to achieve, after all, God is love and chose us first.

> Just "as he chose us in him, before the foundation of the world, to be holy and

> without blemish before him." (Ephesians 1:4a)

> "It was not you who chose me, but I who chose you and appointed you to go and bear fruit that will remain, so that whatever you ask the Father in my name he may give you." (John 15:16)

David's words in Psalm 139 express so beautifully just how intimately the Lord knows us. These words can be on the lips and in the heart of every believer:

LORD, you have probed me, you know me:
you know when I sit and stand;
you understand my thoughts from afar.
You sift through my travels and my rest;
with all my ways you are familiar.
Even before a word is on my tongue,
LORD, you know it all.
Behind and before you encircle me
and rest your hand upon me.
Such knowledge is too wonderful for me,
far too lofty for me to reach.
Where can I go from your spirit?
From your presence, where can I flee?
If I ascend to the heavens, you are there;

if I lie down in Sheol, there you are.
If I take the wings of dawn
and dwell beyond the sea,
Even there your hand guides me,
your right hand holds me fast.
If I say, "Surely darkness shall hide me,
and night shall be my light"—
Darkness is not dark for you,
and night shines as the day.
Darkness and light are but one.
You formed my inmost being;
you knit me in my mother's womb.
I praise you, because I am wonderfully made;
wonderful are your works!
(Psalm 139:1a-14a)

This praise in the heart of David is truly universal. We can understand in a new way that everything God created as spelled out in Genesis, was good, including us! In fact, God is joyous with all of His creation, but He is particularly joyful with His creation of man. Man is the only creation that He gives His image, likeness, and breath. This is truly reason to praise.

"By praise, the Spirit is joined to our spirits to bear witness that we are children of God, testifying to the only

Son in whom we are adopted and by whom we glorify the Father." (CCC 2639)

Praise is an act of participating in the family of God, the triune Godhead, Father, Son, and Holy Spirit. This is quite a profound statement. As we praise we acknowledge each Divine Person of the Trinity in a unique way which is cause for shouting Alleluia—literally the highest word of praise meaning "Praise God."

Several things happen when we praise. First, when we praise, we are joined to the Holy Spirit. Alleluia! Second, we bear witness or testify to the Son who we are, adopted heirs. Alleluia! Finally, when we praise, we glorify the Father. Alleluia! We give glory to the Father!

> "He destined us for adoption to himself through Jesus Christ, in accord with the favor of his will." (Ephesians 1:5)
>
> "For you did not receive a spirit of slavery to fall back into fear, but you received a spirit of adoption, through which we cry, 'Abba, Father!'" (Romans 8:15)

When reading this I get such a vivid image of our Heavenly Father, Daddy, who never tires of opening His arms to us, to embrace us, to accept us where we are, and to accept our praises to Him.

> "Praise embraces the other forms of prayer and carries them toward him who is its source and goal: on God, the Father, from whom are all things and for whom we exist." (CCC 2639)

When I first read this statement, I was really taken aback by the real necessity and power of praise. I imagine praise as a huge, warm blanket where all other prayers come to rest. The other forms of prayer in addition to Praise—Blessing and Adoration, Prayer of Petition, Prayer of Intercession, and the Prayer of Thanksgiving. (See CCC Part Four, Section One, Chapter One, Article 3) This blanket—Praise—is bundled up, protecting and covering all other prayer and, upon reaching the Throne Room of Grace, it is waved before the Father; where all of our prayers are within His reach and answer.

Chapter 2
Expressions of Praise

Non-Verbal Praise

According to Scripture, there are many different ways to express praise to God. The Lord who made us desires for our entire being not only to belong to Him in heart and mind, but to demonstrate our love for Him. Exploring praise as a progression (moving from least to most demonstrative) allows us to consider a form of prayer that may not be considered praise by some: silence. Many things are battling for our attention today and it seems we have become most comfortable as a society to the noise of the day. Real silence has become nonexistent. In the times we live, we are only silent when in front of a screen. Our communication has changed drastically with the fast-paced world of technology. Texting and emails have taken the place of people meeting face to face or having a conversation by phone. While utilizing technology is of great benefit, nothing can take the place of a personal encounter. This is really the heart of who we are as a people of God: chosen, loved, and continually pursued by the Lord for personal encounter.

Have you ever been in a conversation with others that you disagree with or felt that your comments might stir controversy? Instead of responding in words, you respond in silence. In some instances, silence says something that words cannot.

In the spiritual realm, our silence says something to God, and it is an opportunity to allow Him to say something to us. It is a blessing for those who have the grace to be silent before the Lord, purposely and in solitude. Not just a silence for the sake of silence; but a holy silence that allows our sense of the awe of God to have space in our prayer life.

As Catholics, we have many opportunities to praise God in silence. There are times during the Mass when the most appropriate response is silence. We also have opportunities to adore the Lord in silence during the Eucharistic procession or adoration of the Blessed Sacrament. We are also encouraged to be silent before the Lord in our daily prayer time. These planned times of silence are considered prayers of praise just as much as singing a joyful song unto the Lord because we humble ourselves and honor God for who He is. The prescription for praise is not dependent on sound, or gesture; however, I believe there is a time and a place for both. Our heart is the true center of who we are and our words and gestures are a depiction of our heart. The Psalmist puts it so beautifully:

> "Silence is praise to you, Zion-dwelling God, And also obedience. You hear the prayer in it all." (Psalm 65:1-2, The Message)

> "For God alone my soul waits in silence; from him comes my salvation. He alone is my rock and my salvation, my fortress; I shall not be greatly shaken." (Psalm 62:1-2, ESV)

As a child around the age of ten, I remember my grandpa playing hymns on a very small organ that he kept in his room. It was a pastime for him, as he found such pleasure in music. He allowed us to experiment with his organ; often we created only noise, but he encouraged us to practice and play each time we visited. I'm not sure if the hymn *Silent Night* was his favorite or simply the easiest to play, but I specifically remember each time he sat to play it was *Silent Night*—whether Christmas or summer. It's an interesting concept—singing about silence. I think about that hymn and the fact that on the night of Jesus' birth, it would not have been a silent night at all. All the Heavens were rejoicing, the angels were announcing the birth of the Messiah with singing and jubilation. Yet, it was a night that may have birthed holy awe, and silence would have been an appropriate response as well. There is much to be appreciated in the various ways our hearts are moved to praise God. The good news is that the Lord accepts them all.

Verbal Praise

Children from a very young age are encouraged to make sounds and speak in order to communicate and express feelings. Have you ever witnessed grown, dignified people making baby sounds to infants? Grandparents are especially motivated when it comes to this. It's quite interesting to hear such strange sounds not to mention the facial expressions that accompany them! Thus, we have older folks becoming like little children all over again.

We teach toddlers to remember things with rhymes and songs with the aim of developing good language skills. We have them read aloud in classrooms, memorize poetry, deliver speeches, and join debate clubs all in hopes of developing a love of language and reading to expand their knowledge. Our verbal skills become very powerful tools in navigating our futures. It is no different with the Lord; except He is our future. He desires our verbal skills to be developed to communicate with Him and about Him to others. God desires that some of our verbal ability be reserved specifically to give Him praise.

Teach me, LORD, your way
that I may walk in your truth,
single-hearted and revering your name.
I will praise you with all my heart,
glorify your name forever, Lord my God.
(Psalm 86:11-12)

Singing Praise

Music is a part of every culture. Henry Wadsworth Longfellow once said that music is the universal language of mankind. Once, I was in Brazil for a religious event and experienced praise which included music in Portuguese. Although I don't speak Portuguese, the music and singing had a profound effect on me. I remember hearing one song in particular that I immediately felt affection for. It was not just the melody. I could sense something different in the mood and demeanor of the people as they sang. It was as if joy came over their faces expressing a deep sense of rejoicing. Most people were singing out freely and were invigorated with the lyrics and tempo of the song. I could feel myself entering into this atmosphere of joy and praise even though I knew none of the words. About midway through the song, our host and interpreter, told me that this song was written to honor our Our Lady. She began to tell me some of the words to the song. It was actually the words of the Prayer of Consecration to Our Lady put to music and every Brazilian there was familiar with it! After learning of the song's origin, it made me realize why I was experiencing the sweetness of the Spirit and such joy in an atmosphere of praise as Our Lady evokes both joy and praise.

Music is not only cultural but a natural part of some of the most important events in our lives. Weddings, graduations, religious services, funerals, etc… usually include music and it's hard to imagine these occasions without songs being sung to enrich the celebration. It is no different with praise of God. It too should be a natural part of our lives both enriching our celebrations of the Lord whether in community or in our personal time of prayer. Many shy away from singing of any kind because they feel uncomfortable with the way they sound or somehow think their singing is just not good enough. Praise has nothing to do with how lovely we sound; however, it has everything to do with offering our hearts to God. Our singing to God always sounds pleasing to Him; after all He did create our voices and knew very well what He was doing. There are many Scriptures that encourage singing to the Lord. I believe the Psalms provide a starting point, or invitation to sing, but as I once read, not all of the Psalms have been written. This means that there are some in our own hearts that the Lord desires to hear.

"I will sing to the LORD all my life;
I will sing praise to my God while I live."
(Psalm 104:33)

"Give thanks to the LORD, invoke his name;
make known among the peoples his deeds!
Sing praise to him, play music;
proclaim all his wondrous deeds!
Glory in his holy name;
let hearts that seek the LORD rejoice!"
(Psalm 105:1-3)

Singing praise to God is really a way to be lifted up when we are down. It's a way to change our countenance and remind ourselves of our destiny. We are joining our voices with those who have reached their heavenly reward.

All those who "having come through the great tribulation," prophets, saints, intercessions of the witnesses (martyrs) "have gone before us into the Kingdom, [they] all sing the praise and glory of him who sits on the throne, and of the Lamb. In communion with them, the Church on earth (that's us!) also sings these songs with faith in the midst of trial." (CCC 2642) Thus, our faith is pure praise. St. Bernard said, "There is nothing on earth, which so completely represents to us the joys of heaven as the joyful songs of those who praise God."

Music as Praise

As a young person, I developed a real love of music. I was fortunate enough to be exposed to several artists and genres of music. Listening to music was pretty much a daily event when I was growing up. Many in my family learned to play a musical instrument and I was on my way to follow suit. My instrument of choice was the flute. At my school, the flute section was filled with my classmates who had had a few private lessons before music instruction began. Naturally, I had some catching up to do. Each section of instruments was situated in a particular way. If you were the best in your section, you sat first and each student sat in position according to ability. As it turns out, I sat in the last seat in the flute section for two years.

It was during the latter part of the second year that things started to look up. To my surprise, I received a trophy at the end of that year for the most improved student. Ironically, the very next year, I received the most outstanding student of all the sections. Maybe it had something to do with my instructor whom I respected as my teacher. He was very kind; yet, a disciplinarian who was very outgoing and had a wonderful sense of humor. Maybe it was the course requirement of practicing that helped me.

My instructor required each musician to have a practice report. Each day you were to record the amount of minutes you spent practicing, have it signed by your parents, and then return the report for grading each week. Music for me was more than my desire for the good grade. I believe something inside of me wanted to express itself both beautifully and freely. I believe this to be true of all people. There is something inside of us that desires to express itself. But even more than an expression of beauty, it is an expression of truth. I believe this is the part of each person that longs to express belonging, hope, unity, and, most of all, love. This is the part of us that longs to find our "voice;" our satisfaction. It is not dependent on education or wealth, social status, or church affiliation. This is the interior part of us that longs for something and that something is a person—Jesus.

I consider it a great privilege to have had an opportunity to learn to read music and play an instrument. Also, to be instructed by teachers who really cared about the development of the whole person and not just the musical ability.

I see praise closely related to the evolvement of my learning to play an instrument. When I began, I did not know how to play effectively in different keys; however, I practiced and practiced some more, then I became proficient. Praise follows the same pattern. At first, on our own, we may not have many different styles of praising; then we practice and practice praising some more. Then we become more gifted praisers.

Saint Augustine wrote in *Confessions*: "You are Great, O Lord, and greatly to be praised; great is your power, and of your wisdom is without measure … You yourself encourage him to delight in your praise, for you have made us for yourself, and our heart is restless until it rests in you."[11]

There is the part of us that longs to give praise to God, by offering unto Him our abilities. Whether natural or learned, we give back to God, what He freely gives to us. I remember the first time I heard the 8-fold Alleluia. It was not even in a church or at an event sponsored by a church. At 12 years old, that melody of the Alleluia captivated my heart. I liked it the moment I heard it. It was not a song sung at the church that I attended. In fact, I did not hear that song again until I attended a Catholic Charismatic prayer meeting many years later. My heart again was moved. I was longing to express what was happening inside of me. At the time, I could probably only express how much I really liked the song but it was really deeper than just liking a song. It was a melody that I felt took me to a holy place. It was a tune that I never tired of and still don't. I may not have known it at the time, but in reality, I was singing the highest word of praise unto God—Alleluia; which translated from Hebrew means, "praise the Lord!" I was praising God and didn't know it was praise! This is how God can come into our lives in a subtle and unplanned way. He touches us when we are in the midst of our own planned activities. I believe it was no accident to hear that great chorus of praise, the Alleluia. I am so glad that I had ears to hear a one-word song; the highest word of praise used in Scripture and still used today to honor God just because he's God. To that I say, Alleluia!

Praising in the Spirit

Where is all of this praise coming from? The heart. "The heart is our hidden center…only the Spirit of God can fathom the human heart and know it fully." (CCC 2563) If only the Spirit of God can know our hearts fully, then it is only the Spirit of God in us that can praise Him most purely. This is really a point to ponder on many fronts.

First, the fact that the Spirit of God lives in you and me as baptized Christians. Part of the triune Godhead, the Holy Spirit is pure gift to us, living inside of us even in our sinfulness. Second, the Holy Spirit living in us longs to give praise to God the Father through us. One way to do this is through the use of the spiritual gifts. One of the gifts of the Holy Spirit listed in 1 Corinthians 14 is the gift of tongues.

> There are different kinds of spiritual gifts but the same Spirit; there are different forms of service but the same Lord; there are different workings but the same God who produces all of them in everyone. To each

> individual the manifestation of the Spirit is given for some benefit. To one is given through the Spirit the expression of wisdom; to another the expression of knowledge according to the same Spirit; to another faith by the same Spirit; to another gifts of healing by the one Spirit; to another mighty deeds; to another prophecy; to another discernment of spirits; to another varieties of tongues; to another interpretation of tongues. But one and the same Spirit produces all of these, distributing them individually to each person as he wishes. (1 Corinthians 4-11)

There are many teachings promoting the gift of tongues. Some pray in the Spirit and exhort of its value and others conclude that "it's not for me." I would simply like to recall some important truths regarding the gifts. For starters, the Word of God is living and the gifts of God are good. Plain and simple we are told by Saint Paul not to be ignorant of such things (see 1 Corinthians 12:1). We know that tongues is listed as one of the gifts of the Holy Spirit and all of the gifts are encouraged by Saint Paul.

I must confess, for many years I did not fully hear the Word of God nor St. Paul's wisdom when it came to the gifts of the Holy Spirit, including the gift of tongues. I had no preconceived ideas of this gift as I had never given it much thought until I witnessed others praying in tongues or praying "in the Spirit." I concluded that this was a strange sounding way to pray. Since I had never heard or experienced anyone pray by using the gift of tongues, I thought it was very strange. I felt uncomfortable and didn't want to be around such prayer. Then of course came the questioning. *Why have I not heard of this gift until now? How does this benefit me or anyone else? Do I really have to pray this way? Isn't this something only the disciples and others experienced in the Bible? Is this gift really for our times?* I know many people who have the opposite reaction to this gift. They accept tongues as a gift, never question it, and are able to yield to the gift as if it is second nature. As you just read, it did not happen this way for me but I did eventually yield to the gift of tongues. If you were to ask me why I chose to do this, the answer does not lie in the intellect. It was not because someone had explained it in a way that was acceptable; which can be very helpful. Nor was it because it was the Word of God and I was convinced of this truth as I worked to understand the Scriptures. It was because I witnessed and experienced something undeniable in those who yielded to this gift and exercised it in freedom. In my case, not only was seeing believing, but experiencing the joy of others brought about a thirst and desire in my heart for this gift.

Additionally, this is not a "new" way to pray. It's an ancient way to pray and many who we hold in high regard—Saints and Doctors of the Church—spoke of this gift as jubilation, meaning wordless vocal prayer expressing love or joy of the soul. We see the gift of tongues mentioned many times in Acts in conjunction with the Holy Spirit: see Acts 2, Acts 10:46, and Acts 19:6.

While I am not trying to write a commentary on the gift of tongues, I would like to mention one last scripture which clarifies for me the *how* and *why* of praying in the Spirit. First the *How*. Romans 8:26 states, "In the same way, the Spirit too comes to the aid of our weakness; for we do not know how to pray as we ought, but the Spirit itself intercedes with inexpressible groanings." And since the Catechism of the Catholic Church states that, "The Holy Spirit, the artisan of God's works, is the master of prayer," it would then seem logical that we would desire to seek the Holy Spirit and lend our voice to Him in order to fulfill this scripture. (CCC 741) Let's face it, there are times when we really don't know how to pray as we ought. And even when we think we might know how to best pray in the natural, the Spirit can lead us in a more perfect, supernatural way.

The next verse Romans 8:27 is the *Why*. It states, "And the one who searches hearts knows what is the intention of the Spirit, because it intercedes for the holy ones according to God's will." That means when we pray in the Spirit, we pray in unity with the will of the Father. This mysterious gift of tongues allows us to pray and praise more perfectly because it's the Spirit Himself praying through us.

So how do we praise God? On purpose with, "..sighs too deep for words." And why do we praise Him? With purpose "…according to the will of God."

Gestures

In 2014 the Holy Father, Pope Francis met with members of the Charismatic Renewal from around the world at Olympic Stadium in Rome. I watched the video of this gathering many times, and mostly in thanksgiving for the outpouring of the Holy Spirit and the acknowledgement of this world-wide grace. Much was said on this occasion that has encouraged many to go out as the disciples did, with courage and boldness, and to bring the grace of the Baptism in the Holy Spirit to the whole Church.

For me, the most moving part of the whole event was the witness of Pope Francis. This was not an obligatory event that the Holy Father happened to bless with his presence. It was an event the he participated in and encouraged. When I saw him with his hands raised in praise and then kneeling as the community prayed over him in tongues, I was moved to tears. Here was the Vicar of Christ on earth, participating in praise, and receiving the prayers of the people in humility. I witnessed the Holy Father praising God outside of Mass with hands outstretched in freedom. This gesture said more to me than any book I had ever read or teaching I had ever heard on the subject of praise. He commented on the selection of music as one of his favorites and gave witness to the fact that he, and the community he served in Argentina, prayed in tongues. It is sometimes difficult to testify to others about the freedom, joy, and desire to praise that comes with surrendering to the Holy Spirit because they have not experienced it. On this occasion, there was no denying the authenticity of the move of the Spirit in a Charismatic dimension that is still prevalent in the Church today. This is the witness that should cause us to consider the fact that the Holy Spirit is just as alive now as He was on Pentecost over 2000 years ago and that He is always about something new.

Many Psalms exhort us to lift our hands in praise, but there are other Scriptures that encourage us as well:

> "It is my wish, then, that in every place the men should pray, lifting up holy hands, without anger or argument." (1 Timothy 2:8)

> "Ezra blessed the LORD, the great God, and all the people, their hands raised high, answered, 'Amen, amen!' Then they knelt down and bowed before the LORD, their faces to the ground." (Nehemiah 8:6)

> "Pour out your heart like water before the Lord; Lift up your hands to him for the lives of your children." (Lamentations 2:19b)

Probably the most popular Christian gesture is the prayer of the Sign of the Cross. Another gesture that I was familiar with was striking my chest when praying for mercy. Up until my teenage years I had never experienced anyone offering praise to God by way of gestures except for the Sign of the Cross, striking the chest, and the other gestures I had practiced at Mass such as kneeling, standing, bowing or hands clasped together. These are all important to the Lord. He honors them all when stemming from a heart in sincerity. Since this is what I was accustomed to, naturally every other gesture was considered odd. Being rather introverted and timid, you can imagine my feelings regarding any other type of gesture that didn't follow the prescription of what I had experienced or thought appropriate. I was of the mindset that church was no place for clapping, loud singing, or any other gestures; like lifting hands to God, or even swaying or dancing because I had never experienced such a thing. I must confess that stubbornness and pride were also at work on this account. I used to shudder in church when the congregation would applaud because I felt it inappropriate as it wasn't serious or solemn and it would upset the holy activity in the church.

By the grace of God, I was invited to a Charismatic prayer meeting, where I witnessed for the first time, joyful praise with singing accompanied by lifted hands, swaying, and sincerity. I was very uncomfortable the first few times in this joyful setting. I would have been very happy if those at the meeting would honor God by sitting quiet, not getting too loud or excited, and certainly not praying in a way that was free and independent of a schedule. I was all for a program and no spontaneity. As I have looked back many times over the years at my first impression of praising freely, I see that my interpretation of what it meant to honor God was putting the Holy Spirit in a box as if I were in control of the move of God. I know this was due to my lack of knowledge of Scripture and mostly my personal inability to express myself based on my self-consciousness at the time. This is how you know God has a sense of humor—He is now using me to write this book on the very topic that at one time made me so uncomfortable. Yet another reason to give praise!

Chapter 3
The Festal Shout

We as a Christian people have a powerful history of praise. In the Psalms two Hebrew words are used to express praise of God. Those words are *ruwa,* which means, "to shout" as in Psalm 47:2:

> "All you peoples, clap your hands; shout to God with joyful cries. For the LORD, the Most High, is to be feared, the great king over all the earth."

The other word is derived from it which is *teruwah,* meaning a battle cry or joyous acclamation. This is precisely the form of praise Joshua used at Jericho. The people would respond to the sound of the ram's horn and shout a mighty shout unto the Lord for His ways to be accomplished. This praise is far from a faint response. This was loud praise not simply for the sake of being loud, but loud for the sake of expressing "God is with us!"

Here is a powerful example of praising with purpose: the people of Israel are now led by Joshua, since Moses has died. They are on the precipice of claiming the land promised them by God. The problem is that the land is inhabited by giants and fierce warriors who live in fortified cities. As God promised, He remains with His chosen people and provides a strategic plan to Joshua. He is to have the soldiers march around the city for six days with seven priests carrying ram's horns ahead of the Ark of the Covenant of the Lord. On the seventh they were to march around the city seven times keeping silent until they heard the blast of the ram's horn. At the sound of the horns, the people began to shout a tremendous Festal Shout of praise for God's will to be accomplished on their behalf. With this Festal Shout, the wall crumbled and the Israelites attacked and took the city. The presence of God in an atmosphere of praise provided defeat of the enemies.

This is how God wants to move in our own lives of praise. This is an Old Testament Scripture, and we might feel ourselves far removed from it. Maybe you and I aren't on the battlefield like Joshua, but we too have battles before us. We too have walls that have been built around our hearts blocking us from God. These may be in the form of problems in our families, struggles in the workplace, broken relationships, personal sin that holds us bound, or unforgiveness. God calls us as He called Joshua and the Israelites to trust Him for a strategic divine approach. God has strategic plans for all of us. He wants to collapse the walls that separate us from Him. The tearing down of these walls comes in an atmosphere of praise, where the presence of the Almighty God is with His people. This action of praise gives voice to the heart and proclaims this truth—in the end, the victory is ours! God is on our side; always pursuing us, loving us, and providing for us.

You may also recall what happened with the Ark of the Covenant in 1 Samuel 4:5: "When the ark of the LORD arrived in the camp, all Israel shouted so loudly that the earth shook." When the Ark was venerated, God would manifest His presence in power. The loud cry of praise was a way for the people to welcome the Ark and proclaim God was with them. This type of praise, referred to as battle praise, war cry, Festal Shout, and jubilation, a form of tongues, became the prescription for special liturgical celebrations as we see in the Scripture. The ram's horn became the trumpet as we see in Numbers 29, speaking of the Jewish New Year or the Feasts of Trumpets of our Jewish brothers. Over and over again, we read in the

Psalms encouragement to participate in this joyful noise called praise.

If anyone knew how to praise the Lord it was King David. Before David was officially serving in the role of king, he served as armor bearer and musician to his predecessor, King Saul. Saul made several tactical errors during his kingly reign; which was appointed by God. The main reason for Saul's problems was the condition of his heart. Saul's heart drifted from its righteousness for God. Pride and disobedience caused Saul to fail in his divine appointment, which left Samuel to anoint another chosen by God. As God instructs, Samuel searches for a king among the sons of Jesse. Although many of Jesse's sons are kingly in stature, David the youngest, is chosen because he provides what was lacking in King Saul, a true heart for God. He is an unlikely candidate for this kingly position by his outward appearance, but God saw fit to anoint this small, young, red-headed, shepherd boy because of his inward disposition toward the things of God.

One of the most popular stories in the Bible, David and Goliath, demonstrates God's protection and divine intervention when He has ordained an anointing upon a servant, especially when the heart of the servant responds in humility. We know that the odds were against David, who was small, against the giant Goliath. This battle would only be the beginning of the saga of David's life. His life is threatened multiple times; he engages, not only in battle, but war; he's a fugitive; he marries; he loses a son; and, although his life in danger, God blesses him. David, although called to serve, fight, and honor God from the depths of his heart, has something in common with you and me. We may think that David played such a profound role in salvation history and that we don't come close to his chosen position, much less his kingly anointing; however, the truth is that David loved the Lord. His heart was sold out for God, he was anointed and appointed by God, and was also a sinner like you and me. I am not suggesting that we are like David in the area of sin only. In reality we too are called to love God above all as the first commandment tells us. We too are called to surrender ourselves to God's divine providence, and finally we too are chosen and anointed at baptism and again at confirmation. This is a big deal! We are called to participate in the priestly, prophetic, and kingly role of Jesus, the sinless king of all kings, just as David did.

The Scripture tells of the nature of some of David's sinfulness. If David's sin of adultery wasn't bad enough, he couples it with murder and is still considered a man after

God's own heart. This is because David remained humble, recognized his sin, and cried out to God with abandonment. David's sinful heart was rescued by God's grace. No wonder, David, the great musician, who had a sincere heart for praise of God, is thought to be the author of most of the Psalms, which the Catechism refers to as "The Praises." David had good reason to praise and so do we.

What speaks most profoundly to me about David is that he comes clean and continues to offer praise to God. Obviously, David knew that his heart was the very essence of who he was and that being cast away from the presence of God would be dark and torturous. Most of the Psalms can become our own as we can relate to the circumstances or the feelings of the poet who wrote them. This Psalm is one I could sing regularly as I recognize my own heart condition of sinfulness:

Turn away your face from my sins;
blot out all my iniquities.
A clean heart create for me, God;
renew within me a steadfast spirit.
Do not drive me from before your face,
nor take from me your holy spirit.
Restore to me the gladness of your salvation;
uphold me with a willing spirit.

I will teach the wicked your ways,
that sinners may return to you.
Rescue me from violent bloodshed, God, my saving God,
and my tongue will sing joyfully of your justice.
Lord, you will open my lips;
and my mouth will proclaim your praise.
For you do not desire sacrifice or I would give it;
a burnt offering you would not accept.
My sacrifice, O God, is a contrite spirit;
a contrite, humbled heart, O God, you will not scorn.
(Psalm 51:11-19)

David's musical ability by the world's standard would be perhaps considered a natural talent as he was considered one of the best musicians in the kingdom. Every talent is ultimately from the Lord. After all, He is our Creator and knows everything about us. I also believe everyone has some talent necessary for the building up of the Body of Christ. There is great distinction in a worldly view and spiritual view of talent. Any talent that you or I have surrendered unto the Lord becomes something special—a charism; a gift for the expansion of the Body of Christ. God expects us to use them as such. It is evident that King David exercised his charism of music for the kingdom.

Although David was a warrior, he also went to battle with his charism of music. As an offering to God and as service namely to Saul, David accomplished much with his charism. Before becoming king, when David served as Saul's armor bearer, he was called to play music for Saul. This was not for his enjoyment but for a divine purpose: driving the Enemy away!

> Whenever the spirit from God came upon Saul, David would take the harp and play, and Saul would be relieved and feel better, for the evil spirit would leave him. (1 Samuel 16:23)

Clearly David was not playing secular songs for pleasurable entertainment. David was praising with purpose. David was using praise as a weapon; which caused the evil spirits to flee. This should serve as an example of what we should do when we feel the tactics of Satan coming against us; begin to sing out in praise of God and expect Satan to flee!

David's most dramatic expression of praise takes place before the dwelling place of God, the Ark of the Covenant. Contained in the Ark were Aaron's staff, manna from Heaven, and the Commandments. "When the Ark of the Covenant came into camp, all Israel gave a mighty shout, so that the earth resounded." (1 Samuel 4:5) God saw fit to manifest His presence powerfully when the Ark was venerated, and the Festal Shout was an acclamation of the presence of God among the people. The people had begun to remove their hearts from the act of praise, and their praise became lip service. They began to use the Ark as magic. God allowed the Ark to be taken away. I can only imagine the emptiness and anguish of the people of this time. In His mercy, God allowed the Ark to be recovered. Here is where we see the Festal Shout restored.

David knows God's desire to manifest His presence when the Ark of the Covenant is venerated. God had given specific instructions as to how the Ark was to be constructed and also how the Ark was to be handled and transported. When the Ark was recovered, one of David's servants mishandled the Ark by reaching out and touching it, and he was struck dead! So, David began orchestrating the grand return of the Ark to the temple in Jerusalem. He planned for three months as he wanted to make sure that the return of the Ark to Jerusalem was going to be an appropriate, festive and magnificent celebration of God's presence.

When the Ark was brought to Jerusalem, this is where we see David dancing before the Ark with all his might and with abandonment—naked! David expressed dramatic praise to show that he was solely for God and that his eyes were fixed on the Lord.

The Holy Father, Pope Francis, has commented on this prayer of praise. The Holy Father said, "David's prayer of praise brought him to leave all form of composure and to dance in front of the Lord with all his strength. This is the prayer of praise!" He also said that we should pray "with our whole heart," like David, "even his body prayed with that dance."[12]

The Holy Father then said, "A beautiful question that we can ask ourselves today is: 'How is my prayer of praise going? Do I know how to praise the Lord?"[13] I'm sad to report that for much of my life, I didn't have a prayer of praise. I didn't even realize that I was to be participating in a prayer of praise; even when I went to church. For some reason, I had not realized the meaning of the First Commandment. To me, honoring God; concentrating on God should have led to a demonstration of my praise for Him. What I was doing in my heart and what I was thinking in my head was not being shown in the way that I was living or the things that I deemed appropriate ways to honor God.

But David, as the Holy Father says, gave extravagant praise unto the Lord. And you and I need to give extravagant praise unto the Lord. The Lord had done many things in David's life that would cause David to praise Him. The Lord has done things in our lives, amazing things, that should cause us to praise Him with abandonment. With no fear, with no shame of showing forth that God is who we choose above all. God wants His life to be shared. You and I are His hands and His feet upon the earth today; but we're also His mouthpiece and we're the instrument that should sing His praise.

> "Blessed are the people who know the Festal Shout, who walk, O Lord, in the light of thy countenance; they exult in thy Name all the day; they are exalted in thy righteousness." (Psalm 89:15-16, RSV).

> "Shout joyfully to God, all you on earth; sing of his glorious name, give him glorious praise." (Psalm 66:1)

All you peoples, clap your hands;
shout to God with joyful cries.
For the LORD, the Most High, is to be feared,
the great king over all the earth,
Who made people subject to us,
nations under our feet,
Who chose our heritage for us,
the glory of Jacob, whom he loves.
Selah
God has gone up with a shout;
the LORD, amid trumpet blasts.
Sing praise to God, sing praise;
sing praise to our king, sing praise.
(Psalm 47:2-7)

Chapter 4
The Festal Shout Fulfilled

This brings us to the amazing reality of what happens when Mary becomes the New Ark. Within her is Jesus, the Word made flesh, the high priest and king, and the bread of life. This fulfills that which the Ark contained in the Old Testament. The first recorded encounter of Mary as the New Ark is at her visitation to Elizabeth (and John the Baptist in Elizabeth's womb). Just as King David had an encounter with the Lord and expressed extravagant praise before the Ark of the covenant, so too we will see in this Visitation of Mary to Elizabeth, exuberant praise and an encounter with Jesus.

> When Elizabeth heard Mary's greeting, the infant leaped in her womb, and Elizabeth, filled with the holy Spirit, *cried out in a loud voice* and said, "Most blessed are you among women and blessed is the fruit of your womb." (Luke 1:41-42, emphasis added)

Elizabeth's response is a Festal Shout, a jubilation, an acclamation that the Lord is truly present. Just as the Israelites rejoiced loudly in their communion with God, here we have Elizabeth responding in the same manner.

In keeping with the same ritual for Festal Shouts or battle cries, the sound of the ram's horn or the trumpet remained the signal for a response of festal praise in the presence of the Lord even at the Visitation. Mary's greeting to Elizabeth is the sound of the trumpet and Elizabeth's and John's response are the Festal Shout. Luke does not tell us what Mary's words of greeting were, but we know that they were the cause of Elizabeth and John's extravagant praise for the presence of the Lord was indeed in their midst, and Mary's voice was the cause of their response.

For the first time in all of history, Jesus, the Messiah, is on the earth and in the presence of His people and the response according to Scripture is receptivity and praise. At the sound of Mary's greeting, the praise begins—John the Baptist leaps in the womb. In our day, we would call John *a first responder*. Elizabeth tells us, "for at the moment the sound of your greeting reached my ears, the infant in my womb leaped for joy." (Luke 1:44) Just as David danced before the Ark, now John is dancing before the New Ark of the Covenant.

This scene of the Visitation does not end with Elizabeth and John praising; but it continues to illustrate the important role praise plays in the lives of God's chosen people. After Elizabeth refers to Mary as Blessed and the fruit of her womb as blessed, Elizabeth's prophetic response of praise continues, "And how does this happen to me, that the mother of my Lord should come to me?" (Luke 1:43) In an atmosphere of praise and rejoicing, God reveals things to people. He gives Elizabeth this prophetic utterance. Elizabeth received a Word of Knowledge from the Lord. We know by her words that Elizabeth recognizes exactly who Mary and Jesus are because she uses the words "the mother of my Lord" to address them. Mary upon hearing Elizabeth's words and her testifying of John's leaping, then bursts into the greatest hymn of praise of all time in her Canticle of Praise, the *Magnificat*:

"My soul proclaims the greatness of the Lord;
my spirit rejoices in God my savior.
For he has looked upon his handmaid's lowliness;
behold, from now on will all ages call me blessed.
The Mighty One has done great things for me,

and holy is his name.
His mercy is from age to age
to those who fear him.
He has shown might with his arm,
dispersed the arrogant of mind and heart.
He has thrown down the rulers from their thrones
but lifted up the lowly.
The hungry he has filled with good things;
the rich he has sent away empty.
He has helped Israel his servant,
remembering his mercy,
according to his promise to our fathers,
to Abraham and to his descendants forever."
(Luke 1:46b-55a)

Just as the greeting of Mary was the trumpet call to praise, the words of Elizabeth's prophetic rejoicing now become the trumpet which signals Mary to pray her own Festal Shout of praise in her *Magnificat*.

What does this say to us today? When you and I allow ourselves to be free and to praise the Lord, just as innocent John the Baptist did in the womb of Elizabeth, sanctification happens, because God desires to be with his people. If our hearts are right like David, John, Mary, and Elizabeth, something spectacular is on the precipice of happening. This is important for us to understand because God is calling you and me to be like Mary; to be the trumpet, and to also be praise. God is calling and raising up an army of praisers to know the song of praise and live it.

We too can offer extravagant praise surpassing that of the Old Testament because God dwells with His people today in a most unique way. He promised, "I am with you always." (Matthew 28:20) This happens because we are indeed "clothed with power from on high." (Luke 24:49) God desires for us, like Mary, Elizabeth and John, to be filled with the Holy Spirit. As Baptized Christians, we have the very presence of God living in us! We should praise every day. We should celebrate His Presence living in us with our own Festal Shout of praise in private or public because God dwells within us!

Chapter 5
Powerful Biblical Praise

On the journey of discovering our personal call to praise God, we can be encouraged by those who have experienced God's saving grace through extraordinary praise. The following Scriptures provide evidence of God's power in response to praise.

King Jehoshaphat was the king of Judah, but he was not a perfect king because he had listened to the voice of false prophets. He allowed himself to be misled. Jehoshaphat recognized that he needed to protect Judah. Judah was about to be attacked on all fronts. There was no way that Jehoshaphat was going to win this battle. This was a desperate and dire situation. God in his goodness raised up a prophet, who said to the people, "Do not fear or be dismayed at the sight of this vast multitude, for the battle is not yours but God's." (2 Chronicles 20:15a). Verse 17 goes on to say, "You will not have to fight in this encounter."

Then Jehoshaphat knelt down and put his face on the ground. Everyone else followed suit and worshiped the Lord, and the Levites sang praise to the Lord. Then, after Jehoshaphat had his time of worship, the Lord allowed him to develop a strategic plan in this atmosphere of worship. Jehoshaphat instructed them in what they were going to do: first, they were going to trust in the Lord. He appointed some to sing to the Lord; he appointed some to praise the holy appearance as it went forth. And what they sang were these words that you and I sing today: "Give thanks to the Lord, for his love endures forever." (2 Chronicles 20:21b) At that moment, when they began that jubilant hymn, the Lord laid an ambush against the enemies who were coming against Judah—so much that the enemies were vanquished.

Praise took the enemy out—praise can take the Enemy, Satan, out of our lives. When you and I get on our faces and worship the Son of the Living God, He can give you and I a strategic plan—a plan for battle. The plan for Jehoshaphat included praise and singing. I believe the plan for us when we are in a battle includes our praise and singing, our being completely free in the Lord to honor Him for who He is.

Can you imagine what it was like that this victory, which had been prophesied and proclaimed to the people, was now being accomplished in His power? Imagine the festivity and the praise that took place after the battle when they looked down and could see that everyone had been taken out. The Lord, of course, honored His word and so the people rose up again with their instruments—their harps and trumpets—and praised the Lord when the battle was over. The Scripture tells us that the surrounding lands could hear this praise and so they knew of what the Lord had done and fear of the Lord rose up in them.

I believe this is what happens when you and I experience authentic praise—when authentic praise is happening, when hearts are turned to God, something supernatural happens. Something is stirred in those who witness praise. You and I can be changed in the moment of praise. Our praise can be contagious, because those who hear it are affected by it.

The Scripture also tells us of another time when praise was heard, people were affected, and there was a mighty move of God on behalf of His people. Acts 16 is dear to my heart, because I believe that in this power of praise and being led by the Holy Spirit, God will have victory—He will have His way. This is exactly what happened to Paul and Silas. Paul and Silas were filled with the Holy Spirit, their fear dissipated, and they remained focused on the Lord.

> As we were going to the place of prayer, we met a slave girl with an oracular spirit, who used to bring a large profit to her owners through her fortune-telling. She began to follow Paul and us, shouting, "These people are slaves of the Most High God, who proclaim to you a way of salvation." She did this for many days. Paul became annoyed, turned, and said to the spirit, "I command you in the name of Jesus Christ to come out of her." Then it came out at that moment. When her owners saw that their hope of profit was gone, they seized Paul and Silas and dragged them to the public square before the local authorities. They brought them before the magistrates. (Acts 16:16-20a)

Paul and Silas are beaten and then they are thrown into prison. The guard is instructed to guard the prison securely. Paul and Silas are placed in an inner cell.

> About midnight, while Paul and Silas were praying and singing hymns to God as the prisoners listened, there was suddenly such a severe earthquake that the foundations of the jail shook; all the doors flew open, and the chains of all were pulled loose. When the jailer woke up and saw the prison doors wide open, he drew [his] sword and was about to kill himself, thinking that the

> prisoners had escaped. But Paul shouted out in a loud voice, “Do no harm to yourself; we are all here.” He asked for a light and rushed in and, trembling with fear, he fell down before Paul and Silas. Then he brought them out and said, “Sirs, what must I do to be saved?” And they said, “Believe in the Lord Jesus and you and your household will be saved.” So they spoke the word of the Lord to him and to everyone in his house. He took them in at that hour of the night and bathed their wounds; then he and all his family were baptized at once. He brought them up into his house and provided a meal and with his household rejoiced at having come to faith in God. (Acts 16:25-34)

This means that Paul and Silas were singing loudly unto the Lord. They are praising in the midst of a trial and there is a dramatic move of God, an earthquake, chains are loosed, souls are saved, and faith in God is restored. This is the power of praise. Praise makes unjust situations just. Praise unchains the things in our lives that hold us down. Praise effects those who hear it. In the case of Paul and Silas, it’s possible that the others who heard their praise didn’t join in the praise, but it still had an effect on them.

This speaks clearly of the purpose of our praise; especially when we have been unjustly treated. There are many times in our lives when we have been (and may be) treated unjustly; however, I believe God is still calling us to praise Him, even in those situations. Even when we've been wronged. I believe that our praise in unjust situations serves as a beginning, as an opening up, to the beautiful act of forgiveness. Our praise can lead us to a place where we don't focus on ourselves but on the Lord. When we do focus on the Lord, we become more like Him. We become mercy.

These two Scriptures, Jehoshaphat in battle and Paul and Silas in prison, both give the same message. Praising with purpose accomplishes God's will, and a public witness of praise can affect the hearers. In Jehoshaphat's case fear of the Lord came to those in surrounding towns, in Paul and Silas's case, conversion and restoration.

In the Book of Daniel, we see another example of praise. It takes place during the Babylonian captivity, where Jews were persecuted and held captive by King Nebuchadnezzar, who practiced idolatry. The King, in his wrath, has ordered the three young captives to be thrown into the fiery furnace because they refused to "fall down and worship" the golden idol of King Nebuchadnezzar. When the King found out that they did not follow the order, he gave them a second opportunity to worship the idol. In essence, they were ordered to sin. We can look at being ordered to sin as becoming more and more a problem in our own society today. Mandates are placed in business and healthcare which go directly against the teaching of the Church and infringe on our religious freedom rights. We too will have to choose what voice we will listen to and accept the consequences in the assurance of God's protection.

The astounding response of these three young men is one of total trust and surrender:

> Shadrach, Meshach, and Abednego answered King Nebuchadnezzar, "There is no need for us to defend ourselves before you in this matter. If our God, whom we serve, can save us from the white-hot furnace and from your hands, O king, may he save us! But even if he will not, you should know, O king, that we will not serve your god or worship the golden statue which you set up." (Daniel 3:16-18)

What they are really saying is that they choose martyrdom. They are not intimidated by the king nor are they frightened by the king's utter rage at their response to honor nothing other than God. This is extraordinary faith. As the Catechism tells us, "faith is pure praise." (CCC 2642)

The ending to the story of the three in the fiery furnace gives us great insight and hope. They are bound and thrown into the furnace. They begin to walk in the flames, "singing to God and blessing the Lord." (Daniel 3:24b) Then an intense Canticle of Praise is given by one of the three expressing their sincere position. Nothing can shake their faith, their resolve, and their praise! It's as if there is no earthly fire in the furnace, rather the real fire in the furnace is one of hearts burning with love of God and expressed as praise, contrition, and petition.

Pope Saint John Paul II says of this Scripture, "Nightmares evaporate like mist in sunshine, fears dissolve and suffering vanishes when the whole human being becomes praise and trust, expectation and hope. This is the strength of prayer when it is pure, intense, and total abandonment to God our provident Redeemer."[14]

Not only did the Lord hear them, He delivered them by way of an angel, who not only drove out the flames, but made a "dew-laden breeze" blow. They were in no way harmed or touched by the fire. Not even a hair on their heads were touched, their garments were intact, and they did not even smell of smoke! This is God's complete rescue and protection in response to praise.

Chapter 6
Possibility in Praise

Something happens when we praise and I believe it has everything to do with humility and sincerity of heart. When you and I pray any type of prayer whether silent, spoken, sung, written, or read, we must humble ourselves to do it. Praise requires us to take our eyes off of ourselves and center our attention on the Lord. St. Gregory the Great said, "The joy of the songs of praise turns the eyes of the heart toward heaven." It is right for us to put ourselves aside and focus only on the Lord. We were created to praise. Psalm 102:19 is a prophetic call to praise: "Let this be written for the next generation, for a people not yet born, that they may praise the LORD." Our praise of God was something God intended of us. Praise is not just something we do to fulfill an obligation. Jesus said of the Pharisees, "This people honors me with their lips, but their hearts are far from me;" (Matthew 15:8) Humility is the disposition required of us to properly communicate our heart-felt love for God who desires our affections.

Amazing things happen both physically and spiritually when we praise God. Our hearts, attitudes, dispositions, receptivity, and our capacity for God are affected by our praise. Our hearts are softened and become more docile to the things of God. We place ourselves in a position of receptivity and surrender allowing us to create a pathway to receive more of the Holy Spirit. We have greater capacity for the multiple outpourings of the Holy Spirit. And with all of this, comes joy. Even if we're praising through a tough situation, we choose to praise as we know we praise not for the difficulty of the situation, but for the good that God wants to bring of it. We know that victory is ours in the end so we praise through it.

There is power in our praise. We move from the natural to the supernatural. Divinity and humanity are in communion. The atmosphere is changed because as Scripture is sometimes interpreted, "The Lord inhabits the praise of his people." (Psalm 22:3)

When we praise, there is opportunity for breakthrough, healing, and miracles. We have seen some extraordinary things happen in the Scripture when the people of God praise. Battles are won, walls tumble, there are earthquakes, prison doors are opened, and chains are loosed. These are extraordinary effects of praise, which confirms that we should expect the unexpected when we "worship in spirit and truth." (John 4:24)

There are also other personal benefits that happen in an atmosphere of praise. The Gifts of the Holy Spirit begin to flow in an atmosphere of praise. Thus, the reason why we begin most prayer gatherings in praise is because our praise stirs up the gifts of the Holy Spirit. The Body of Christ, that's us, is ministered to in the will of the Father through people who are operating in the gifts of the Holy Spirit. The gifts of prophecy, word of knowledge, healing, tongues, interpretation of tongues, wisdom, and miracles are for us, to build one another up in the power of the Holy Spirit.

Burdens are replaced with joy. Anxiety is replaced with peace. We begin to see as He sees and we are refreshed. Praise can change our demeanor. There are no limits with God! No human invented praise. Praise was always the divine plan of God. Happy are we who have ears to hear, (ref. Matt 11:15) and hearts to participate.

Praise drives the Enemy away. The Enemy cannot stand it when we praise God. Not because he doesn't like the things of God, but because he wants them for himself. Lack of humility is the reason Satan, engaged in battle with

St. Michael. He basically said, *I will not serve*. Which can also be interpreted, *I will not praise*. Satan and a third of the angels were cast out of Heaven and down to the earth because of pride. Pride is the opposite of humility; which means praise is in direct contradiction of Satan. Another reason why Satan can't stand our praise of God is because he has experience with the praise of God and he knows its intensity and power. He once belonged to the praise community of Heaven as we know he was Lucifer, light-bearer, whom theologians believe was from one of the highest choruses of angels. He understands the effects of praise and he will do anything and everything to cause us not to praise. One of his main tactics is discouragement. If we just become distracted and begin to focus only on our problems, we soon begin to live outside of joy.

The Enemy is trying to seduce society into negative and selfish attitudes. It says this, "I'm not feeling it." It's as if we are allowing ourselves only to move in the direction of our feelings, which are neither right nor wrong—they are feelings. It doesn't matter how we feel; we praise because the Word says to do it and we know God desires it, but most importantly, because He's worthy of our praise. I'm not suggesting we live in denial. The reality is that some of us have situations that can bring us to a place of desperation but we can combat our desperation with the weapon of praise. Our prayerful response to our situations will lead us out of them. God longs for us to be in communion with Him no matter how we feel. Praise helps us get there.

Difficulty in Praise

I love looking at old photographs. It's fascinating to see how we've changed and yet how some things remain unchanged. Also intriguing are the physical characteristics and resemblance of relatives. Certain features are so dominant in some families that when you see a person, you can say he or she is a (say the given last name). However, what seems to also get attention are the hairstyles and fashion. Whether plaid pants, dark rimmed glasses, bushy hair, or no hair, often there is a hearty laugh when we look back at the past. Maybe you've said this line when looking at old photographs, "This was in style back then!" Somehow being "in style" whether intentional or not, justifies the look, and the laugh.

I imagine myself taking a photograph of Heaven. It would be the same "shot" each day. If you can imagine with me, what would that picture look like? I see a joyous people; a satisfied people praising God. A people whose

God is the only object of their desire. The beatific vision, the face of God, now a visible reality. It is interesting that in the Catacombs, the earliest depictions of faith, that none are kneeling. Most have hands raised to God including Our Lady. I am not demoting praying on our knees in any way; however, there are many different postures for praising God prayerfully. To see a picture of praise in our minds sometimes helps us to understand that it's really all right to praise God in such a way here on earth. In fact, when we do, God honors and accepts it. It's a *todah*, a thank offering unto the Lord. A gift in return for all He has done, but mainly for all He is.

Some people by nature are more demonstrative and have no problem lifting hands. It seems to come natural to some, while for others it may be a struggle. I know people who are very introverted, yet when it comes to praising God, you would never know it. I also know others who are extroverted; yet have never thought of raising hands to God as an offering. We can point to our upbringing, our religious affiliation, or simply what we feel comfortable with as to why we do or do not feel comfortable raising our hands unto the Lord in praise. I say this because I was one of those people who didn't particularly think raising hands was necessary; nor did I feel comfortable around others who were praising, because I had not yet acknowledged God's great love for me and that all that I am, and all that I possess, are due to Him and Him alone.

Unlike our old photographs, praise is always "in style" and always appropriate. I can't think of a time when praise is not appropriate. I once attended a funeral of a dear friend of mine's mother. This funeral was considered a home-going, a celebration of her life upon her death. The Gospel choir was singing and people were joining in the praise of God. This was not uncommon for the many funerals I had attended at this church. I had a real awakening while sitting in the church and observing the immediate family of the deceased parishioner. At one point in the service, the choir began to sing a song recorded by The Georgia Mass Choir titled, "I Still Have a Praise." Some of the words are:

I been through the fire and
I been through the flood
Broken in pieces
and left all alone
But through it all God blessed me
and through it all God kept me
and I still have a praise inside of me.
Let me tell you what my praise is.
There is a praise in my spirit

a praise down in my soul
a glory hallelujah
that cannot be controlled
and I still have a praise inside of me.
Hallelujah
Hallelujah
Lord, I love you
Lord, I love you.

Upon hearing the first few words of this song, the family of the deceased stood to their feet, raising their hands and swaying to the music in praise of God. Even in the midst of such sorrow and emotion, here was a family who loved God and praised God in one of the most difficult days of their lives, saying farewell and burying their mother. I witnessed firsthand people who knew and trusted God and understood that praise is always due Him, no matter what. I was so moved by this and my heart was singing its own song of praise as I realized God was letting me see the subject of this book—*praise!*— in action. I sat there thinking to myself: how is it that people who love God so much, even in good times, struggle to praise God with such beauty and abandonment, and these people are praising Him during one of the most difficult times with such passion and freedom and faith?

At the end of the service, one line of this song took root in my heart, "*there's a glory hallelujah that I just cannot control.*" It's become like an anthem for me; praise is on the agenda for my life. My motto would become: "praise in all circumstances." I have experienced the power of praise as I praised God through the storms of my own life. But seeing this vision of praise of a people unshaken by death, poised with passion and supernatural strength, I left this home-going celebration with a new depth of understanding the appropriateness to praise God in all situations.

A Visitation of Praise

Although we are called to be a joyful people, life's circumstances can cause us to forget that call. All of us experience painful situations which may cause us to say those famous words, "Life isn't fair." No one is immune to pain and suffering. It may come in different forms, but let's face it, pain and suffering are a part of the cross we carry due to the sinful nature of man. Our cross is not dependent upon the amount of sin or our lack of sin. I, like you, have experienced my own pain and suffering. At one point in my life, I was in such a desperate situation, a very dark time, that even my family and friends that were closest to me could not console me. I ran to the Tabernacle, as I deemed it the only place safe, my only consolation. I had thoughts of bringing my sleeping bag into the church and spending the night there, at the foot of the Tabernacle where I knew I would be safe and secure. I didn't do that, but it was my initial thought process; to find a respite, at such a dark moment.

All I could do was weep. I had nothing left in me to offer the Lord but my tears. Something incredible began to happen. I saw my tears washing over the nail prints on the feet of Jesus. My tears were washing His feet! I felt caught up in something supernatural. As I continued to offer myself to the Lord in all my brokenness, I again saw something incredible. I began to see myself with Jesus. We were standing face to face. And in the midst of all those tears, it's as if Jesus was giving me an opportunity for joy! I saw Him place Himself Eucharistically into my heart, as if my heart were His new home. And then, even more joy came when I saw Him place His hands extended in such a position as if to ask me for a dance. Jesus, a perfect gentlemen! Only the Lord, who knows every intimate detail about us, would ask me to do something that brought me such joy in the midst of great tribulation.

What I have come to know through this experience is that even our tears can be offered as praise unto God. I was before the Tabernacle, before the Body, Blood, Soul, and Divinity of Jesus, truly present, offering Him all I had…pain. I believe my offering of tears was accepted, not because of me, or my situation, but rather because of who I brought them to, the source of our true consolation, Jesus the King of Kings. I didn't realize it at the time, but what I was doing was actually placing myself under his Lordship and that is praise! I was literally, crying out to God, and that's praise too. I didn't come into the full knowledge of what had happened during this personal encounter until I began to meditate on the following Scripture:

> A Pharisee invited him to dine with him, and he entered the Pharisee's house and reclined at table. Now there was a sinful woman in the city who learned that he was at table in the house of the Pharisee. Bringing an alabaster flask of ointment, she stood behind him at his feet weeping and began to bathe his feet with her tears. Then she wiped them with her hair, kissed them, and anointed them with the ointment. When the Pharisee who had invited him saw this he said to himself, "If this man were a prophet, he would know who and what sort of woman this is who is touching him, that she is a sinner." Jesus said to him in reply, "Simon, I

> have something to say to you." "Tell me, teacher," he said. "Two people were in debt to a certain creditor; one owed five hundred days' wages and the other owed fifty. Since they were unable to repay the debt, he forgave it for both. Which of them will love him more?" Simon said in reply, "The one, I suppose, whose larger debt was forgiven." He said to him, "You have judged rightly." Then he turned to the woman and said to Simon, "Do you see this woman? When I entered your house, you did not give me water for my feet, but she has bathed them with her tears and wiped them with her hair. You did not give me a kiss, but she has not ceased kissing my feet since the time I entered. You did not anoint my head with oil, but she anointed my feet with ointment. So I tell you, her many sins have been forgiven; hence, she has shown great love. But the one to whom little is forgiven, loves little." He said to her, "Your sins are forgiven." The others at table said to themselves, "Who is this who even forgives sins?" But he said to the woman, "Your faith has saved you; go in peace." (Luke7:36-50)

Although I was not lavishing the Lord in a public setting, nor did I have an alabaster jar of perfumed oil, in His mercy, I believe the Lord did see my heart just as He had seen this woman's. He overlooked my sinfulness and accepted my offering.

This episode in Scripture takes place just before Jesus' triumphant entry into Jerusalem; which is the cause of much celebration and praise in the Jewish culture. It was a very intimate act of praise that foreshadowed the destiny of Jesus. A young girl, who was "known" in the town, had a reputation, and she was not a wholesome, chaste, woman. She is criticized for lavishing Jesus with very expensive perfumed oil as she washes his feet with her tears, and dries them with her hair. This is an example of personal and extravagant praise, that, in her case, went beyond her reputation. It was praise that came from a heart ready to give God glory in a way that seemed inappropriate to those around her.

First, the timing of this act may have seemed out of order because Jesus is reclined at table with others. Second, she is a woman. Then, there's the issue that it was considered extremely wasteful to break open the alabaster jar of oil that would have been worth 300 days wages. Even more appalling than wasting all the oil, was who was doing the wasting. It was lavished upon Him not by a commoner, but by a woman whose sinfulness was great. I suspect she would have been the woman in the town that would have been the subject of many whispered conversations. I am so moved by this extravagant act of praise because she pulls out all the stops despite her sinfulness. Maybe there was an unknown reason for her lifestyle. Poverty and brokenness can cause us to behave in a way that brings us to moments of desperation. Yet she recognizes Jesus as her personal king. Even though washing feet is customary in the Jewish culture of Jesus' time, He points out that no one else has washed His feet on this occasion, nor given Him a drink.

Those in attendance were focused on what they could see in the natural. Jesus saw beyond the drama; He saw a woman with a sincere and contrite heart ready to praise and honor her king. Her humility overshadowed her sin. Without reservation, He gave her the privilege to wash His feet: to offer praise to God, because He is God.

You and I might look at this scene and think that it is unreasonable for the others in attendance to judge her in this manner; after all, she is washing the feet of the King. This exemplifies the eyes on which the Lord looks upon us. Eyes that see beyond what even our actions say about us, eyes that see the very source of who we are, our heart. The heart, the place that the Catechism of the Catholic Church says is the very part of us that praises God. It is the whole man who prays, but it is the heart, stated over 1000 times in Scripture as the source of it. (ref. CCC 2562)

Chapter 7
Masterwork of Praise

The prayer of the Psalms is always sustained by praise; that is why the title of this collection as handed down to us is so fitting: "The Praises." (CCC 2589)

Of all the books in the Bible, there is something unique about the Book of Psalms. Written as songs, in the style of poetry, and sometimes set to music, the Psalms express the heart of the writer and have great influence as they express relatable human experiences. While the writing of the Psalms is mainly attributed to King David, there are other writers mentioned as well. According to the Catechism of the Catholic Church, there are some truths about the Psalms which may help us better understand the role and function of this treasury of prayer.

The Psalms are considered the prayers of the people of God. It's interesting to note that the Psalms both "nourished and expressed the prayers of the People of God," (CCC

2586) and at the same time are the "masterwork of prayer in the Old Testament." (CCC 2585)

When praying the Psalms, we enter the heart and feel the conviction of the writer under the influence of the Holy Spirit. The Psalms illustrate the passion of the writer for which there is no substitute. This gives reason to St. Paul's encouragement, "addressing one another [in] psalms and hymns and spiritual songs, singing and praying to the Lord in your hearts, giving thanks always and for everything in the name of our Lord Jesus Christ to God the Father." (Ephesians 5:19-20)

The Psalms comprise a wide variety of prayer, expressing emotions, from thanksgiving to lamenting, from crying out for mercy to proclaiming His victory, from contrition to jubilant rejoicing, from vengeance and justice to forgiveness and peace. The Book of Psalms includes a prayer for the condition of every human heart. Most importantly, the Psalms were "prayed by Christ and fulfilled in him." (CCC 2586)

"Certain constant characteristics appear throughout the Psalms: simplicity and spontaneity of prayer……..in the certitude of his love and in submission to his will." (CCC 2589) This is a statement of hope for us as I believe this is precisely what the Lord desires of us: To express our condition and place them before the Lord in simplicity, without worry of elaborate wording, but also in spontaneity, absent of a prescribed ritualistic formula, and totally the expression of a pure heart.

A sense of commonality and relationship exists between author and reader. As we hear the voice of the Psalmists who express deep affection for God, we see them along a spectrum of emotion as crying out to God in times of temptation and trouble, and at the same time emphasizing an overwhelming awe and trust in the Lord that often concluded in exuberant rejoicing. The Psalms are an explicit example of a human being willing to offer ultimate heart-exposure in abandonment to its Creator. The words of the Psalms not only guide us and teach us to pray, but can be made into our own hymn of the heart.

Many of the Psalms have been quoted in this book and still there are many others. The Book of Psalms is the longest book of the Bible, and contains 150 Psalms.

The very last Psalm is like the Grand Finale ending in a great crescendo of praise; with volume and intensity because it calls musicians and dancers to lead all on earth and in Heaven to praise the Lord. The last verse of the final Psalm is: “Let everything that has breath give praise to the Lord! Hallelujah!” (Psalm 150:6)

How did our breath come to be? What distinguishes our breath from every other living thing that breathes? The answer goes back to the second story of creation in Genesis, Chapter 2. "Then the LORD God formed the man out of the dust of the ground and blew into his nostrils the breath of life, and the man became a living being." (Genesis 2:7) Simply put, our breath is His breath. Man breathes with the breath of God. When we offer words of praise to God, we give back to God what was originally His. But even more profound than offering our words as praise is offering the simplest praise, that is our breathing.

We are the only creature that breathes that can make the decision to praise God. All others give praise to God by their existence but we praise God by our existence, our reflection of His image, and our will. There is a beautifully written song titled "Your Grace Finds Me" by Matt Redman. It was produced by Sixstepsrecords and Sparrow Records in 2013. It reminds me of what a modern-day Psalm would sound like. Its chorus says, "I'm breathing in your grace and breathing out your praise." When I first heard these lyrics, I thought to myself, *That's it!* Breathing is one of our earliest expressions of praise. We give Him honor with our God-given breath.

In a nutshell, Psalm 150 tells us: everything, everywhere, is called to praise God using every possible means. Pope Saint John Paul II says Psalm 150, "sets a spiritual seal on the whole Psalter, the book of praise, of song, of the liturgy of Israel." He also acknowledges that, "the Psalmist urges us to find help for our praise in the prayerful encounter; sound the musical instruments of the orchestra of the temple of Jerusalem, such as the trumpet, harp, lute, drums, flutes and cymbals."[15]

Why such extravagant praise at the end of the Psalms? It's because of *what* He does, has done, and will do; and *who* He is.

St. Basil the Great, Doctor of the Church and father of Eastern Monasticism, wrote a commentary titled, "The Psalms: Voice of the Church and Medicine for Hearts." In it he explains the Psalms as a "Pharmacy open to all souls." He sums up precisely our reason for remaining close to the Psalms.

> But the Book of Psalms contains everything useful that the others have. It predicts the future, it recalls the past, it gives directions for living, and it suggests the right behavior to adopt. It is, in short, a jewel case in which have been collected all the valid teachings in such a way that individual find remedies just right for their cases. It heals the old wounds of the soul and gives relief to recent ones. It

> cures the illnesses and preserves the health of the soul.[16]

St. Ambrose of Milan, one of the four original Doctors of the Church, gives us a poetic portrayal of the Psalms.

> What is a Psalm but a musical instrument to give expression to all the virtues? The Psalmist of old used it, with the aid of the Holy Spirit, to make earth re-echo the music of heaven. He used the dead gut of strings to create harmony from a variety of notes, in order to send up to heaven the song of God's praise. In doing so he taught us that we must first die to sin, and then create in our lives on earth a harmony through virtuous deeds, if the grace of our devotion is to reach up to the Lord.[17]

It is right for us to consider these words of St. Ambrose as he puts a condition on our prayers of praise reaching the Lord and our reception of grace. He uses a metaphor describing a Psalm as a musical instrument explicitly describing a "dead gut" meaning something had to die in order to produce the string to create the sound or music. So, too it is with us. We too must die to sin in order to produce music of praise unto the Lord.

St. Augustine of Hippo, who was a student of St. Ambrose and also one of the four original Doctors of the church, gave a sermon on Psalm 149 titled, *Eastertide*.

Psalm 149:1b reads, "Sing to the Lord a new song; his praise in the assembly of the faithful." St. Augustine specifically gave this sermon to the newly baptized as they have become "new men." He says:

> "A song is a thing of joy; more profoundly, it is a thing of love. Anyone, therefore, who has learned to love the new life has learned to sing a new song… The Psalms do not tell us not to love, but to choose the object of our love."[18]

St. Augustine is often misquoted as saying, "He who sings prays twice." His encouragement of singing to the Lord also comes with a challenge. While affirming singing to the Lord is important, he challenges us to also provide the accompaniment by becoming the object of our singing—love itself. Both Augustine and Ambrose bring new meaning and substance to what I once considered legitimate praise. Dying to self and becoming the object of our praise set a precedent for praise. It calls for us striving to be right before God. It calls for an honest examination of our lives. Dying to self means humility and reconciliation.

This final quote from Saint Augustine concisely explains the real meaning behind our praise, the transformation of our lives as the ultimate praise to God.

My dear brothers and sons, fruit of the true faith and holy seed of heaven, all you who have been born again in Christ and whose life is from above, listen to me; or rather, listen to the Holy Spirit saying through me: *Sing to the Lord a new song*…make sure that your life does not contradict your words. Sing with your voices, your hearts, your lips and your lives: *Sing to the Lord a new song'*...If you desire to praise him, then live what you express. Live good lives, and you yourselves will be his praise.[19]

Chapter 8
The Sacrifice of Praise

As I prepare to attend Mass, these are some of the questions that I ask myself. As a people of praise, we can ponder these to deepen our experience of the presence of God at Mass.

> *Do we sing joyfully in expectant faith and thanksgiving for who we are privileged to encounter? Do we welcome the presence of Christ? Are we anticipating that we are preparing to host the presence of God? Are our hearts burning within us to hear the word of God as our brothers experienced on the Road to Emmaus? Are we expecting to witness the greatest miracle, bread and wine become the body and blood of Christ? Do we ask Mary to prepare our hearts to receive her son? Do we place ourselves at the altar along with the monetary offering collected as an offering unto to Lord for service, witness, and sacrifice? Do we*

expect to be encouraged to go out and share the faith with passion?

There is certainly reason to praise God for the rich heritage of faith that belongs to all Christians, none more astounding than what takes place at the Catholic Mass. The Mass offers us an occasion to celebrate, in a most profound way, Jesus offering Himself as the sacrifice to God on behalf of our sinfulness.

There are two main parts to the Mass: Liturgy of the Word and Liturgy of the Eucharist. The word "Eucharist" literally means "thanksgiving." There is a built-in element of praise in the Mass by means of the very word "Eucharist." We are fed from two tables at the Mass: the table of the Word and the table of the Eucharist. The intent is for us to eat from both.

Sadly, many believe that we eat only the Eucharist. We cannot forget the words of John in the Gospel whose main goal is to express that the Word of God is the Son of God. He tells us, "In the beginning was the Word, and the Word was with God, and the Word was God" (John 1:1). The Word is God, living and true in every age. John also tells us, "…the Word became flesh and made his dwelling among us, and we saw his glory, the glory as of the Father's only Son, full of grace and truth." (John 1:14).

There is no question of which is more important or greater, the Word or the Body of Christ. Rather it is an understanding that the Word of God and the Body of Christ belong together. The Word of God is living, and the bread and wine once consecrated are transformed to the Body, Blood, Soul, and Divinity of Jesus, the Living Savior of the World.

We can draw the conclusion that the commonality of the Word and the Eucharist is that they are *living*. But there is someone else also active in both parts of the Liturgy in a special way—the Holy Spirit, the "Lord and Giver of Life" as we proclaim in the creed.

> The Holy Spirit gives spiritual understanding of the Word of God to those who read or hear it, according to the dispositions of theirs hearts. (CCC 1101)
>
> The Epiclesis is the intercession in which the priest begs the Father to send the Holy Spirit, the Sanctifier, so that the offerings may become the body and blood of Christ and that the faithful, by receiving them, may themselves become a living offering to God. (CCC1105)

What a privileged people we are to encounter Jesus in the Word and in the Eucharist, and if Baptized, to experience the indwelling of the Holy Spirit in our very being connecting us to this holy sacrifice. The Holy Spirit is the agent who awakens in us our responsibility to honor God and gives us the grace necessary for us to offer ourselves in service as a living sacrifice of praise to God.

> Christian liturgy not only recalls the events that saved us but actualizes them, makes them present. The Paschal mystery of Christ is celebrated, not repeated. It is the celebrations that are repeated, and in each celebration there is an outpouring of the Holy Spirit that makes the unique mystery present. (CCC 1104)

> The Eucharist contains and expresses all forms of prayer it is "the pure offering" of the whole Body of Christ to the glory of God's name and, according to the traditions of East and West, it is *the* "sacrifice of praise." (CCC 2643)

Of most importance is to first recognize the Mass as ***the*** sacrifice of praise; and second to participate in it fully. I attended Mass regularly, followed the missal, responded verbally, and prayed earnestly during the Liturgy. I can say that I truly did not understand the praise part of the sacrifice. For some reason the words did not match what was to be present in my heart.

Pope Francis delivered some interesting comments regarding the Mass and praise. In his homily (May 2013), he speaks of an attitude of joy that comes from praising God. I found these words of the Holy Father most encouraging. It was the birth of a new yearning in my heart to really praise God freely, especially at Mass!

> "We Christians are not so accustomed to speak of joy, of happiness. I think often we prefer to complain. It's the Spirit that guides us: He is the author of joy, the Creator of joy……Without joy, we Christians cannot become free, we become slaves to our sorrows…….. Often Christians behave as if they were going to a funeral procession rather than to praise God…….And how do we praise God? We praise Him by coming out of ourselves, we praise Him freely, like the grace that He gives us is free.[20]

Wow! There it is. The Holy Father is encouraging us to "praise him freely" and to "come out of ourselves." He then poses a question to those present, and I believe this question can be asked of us today:

> You here at Mass, do you give praise to God or do you only petition God and thank God? Do you praise God? This is something new, new in our spiritual life. Giving praise to God, coming out of ourselves to give praise; spending a little bit of time giving praise.

> But this Mass is so long?' If you do not praise God, you will never know the gratuity of spending time praising God…But if you go with this attitude of joy, of praise to God, that is Beautiful! This is what eternity will be: giving praise to God? And that will not be boring: it will be beautiful![21]

The Holy Father's questions are some we must all ask ourselves. Our preparation for Heaven, our true retirement, has already begun here on earth especially during the Mass. Our retirement requirement: praise. Our participation in the sacrifice of the Mass here on earth is already taking place in Heaven. We join in the unending hymn of praise, *Holy, Holy, Holy…..*

So as not to write a full commentary on the Mass, I would like to give a general overview of our participation of praise during Mass. First, we come together as the Body of Christ and prepare ourselves to listen to the Word of God and to celebrate the Eucharist by standing and singing the processional song. As the priests, deacons, and servers approach the altar, we sing in joyful expectation of a manifestation of the presence of God. The priests and deacons venerate the altar on behalf of all celebrating. The procession reminds me of Jesus' triumphal entry into Jerusalem when the people are crying out, "Hosanna to the Son of David, Blessed is He….Hosanna in the highest. I can picture this scene with palm branches waving about. We, too, welcome Jesus in the person of the priest who stands in *persona Christi*—in the person of Christ.

We then Sign ourselves, are greeted by the priest and acknowledge our sinfulness by praying one of the Penitential Acts in order to "prepare ourselves to celebrate the sacred mysteries." Then the whole church bursts forth in praise, "Glory to God in the highest, and on earth peace to people of good will," echoing the prayer of the angels at the birth of Jesus Christ. (see Luke 2:14)

The Liturgy of the Word begins and it is as if we begin a sacred conversation: hearing the Word of God and responding. The First Reading is read, and we respond in praise, "Thanks be to God." Then the Psalm is read or sung and we again respond as to continue the conversation, but now expressing and making the Psalms the prayer of our own hearts.

The Second Reading is read, and we respond in praise, "Thanks be to God." We then stand and sing the Gospel Acclamation accompanied with the highest word of praise, "*Alleluia!*" to welcome the Gospel, and we remain standing to honor this high point in the Liturgy. The priest or deacon announces the Gospel, and we Sign ourselves and respond in praise, “Glory to you, O Lord.” At the end of the Gospel we reply, “Praise to you, Lord Jesus Christ.”

We then hear the homily, and once it is concluded, again respond in praise—this time by a period of brief silence for recollection. We recite The Creed, the Prayers of the Faithful then, the priest concludes with a short prayer and the Liturgy of the Word is concluded.

If we only look at the response of the congregation in the Mass so far, we see that our responses are mostly responses of praise.

- ✞ We sing a processional song
- ✞ “Glory to God in the highest…”
- ✞ “Thanks be to God”
- ✞ “Alleluia”
- ✞ “Glory to you, O Lord”
- ✞ “Praise to you, Lord Jesus Christ”

So far we can see that this is a very sacred time of praise. It’s a time like no other as we celebrate in community and in communion with God present in his priest, his people and Eucharistically: His body and Blood. It’s not a private time as we are part of the Church, the Body of Christ, but it is a personal time as we are penitent, praiser, and receiver.

The Liturgy of the Eucharist begins with the Offertory. This is when gifts are brought to the altar, blessed and received by the presider of the Mass. This seems appropriate as the only way for us to receive the Eucharist, Jesus in flesh and divinity, is by Jesus first "offering" Himself to God the Father on our behalf. It is right that we give something to God in return for His ultimate sacrifice. This something that we offer could be a variety of things. Each culture has a different way of celebrating the Offertory. While visiting with an African priest, I came to learn that the African custom of the offertory was an opportunity for celebrating and processing by those in the congregation with gifts to offer. Some did so by dancing to the altar to place simple gifts of eggs, fruit, or harvest, or even a chicken. In other cultures, collecting monetary offerings or other gifts for the poor or for the needs of the Church are the custom. Whatever the offering, we are challenged to give what the Holy Spirit will direct us to give; sometimes out of our need.

One particular offering is necessary for the celebration of the Eucharist in any culture. It is the bread and wine for the celebration. Without it, there can be no sacrifice of the Mass. It is here at the offertory that I believe our greatest personal opportunity for giving exists. It goes beyond what we part with to share with others or offer to the Church for its needs. It is our total self-giving unto the Lord. Giving of our material goods is a pious gesture. It takes a person of great faith and trust in the Lord to give out of need. We see this with the widow in the Scripture. Our generosity is a gift, our willingness to part with something as an offering unto the Lord is appropriate for all He has done, is doing, and will do. But there is something in this part of the Liturgy that can become more intense and intimate for us.

It's the realization that Christ totally gave Himself for each one of us in a most profound way, and it is here, along with the bread and wine, that we can offer ourselves to the service of the Lord. It is here that we have a tremendous opportunity, to yearn and cry out to God in our hearts: *Consecrate me that I may become a praise unto you, Lord! Set me apart for you and your works. Enlighten me, Holy Spirit, that I may become all that God has called me to be.*

This may seem like an "elevation of self" in using our imaginations to place ourselves at the foot of the altar as an offering crying-out to God. But I believe it's an opportunity to surrender, to trust, and to exercise Holy Fear. Here we offer ourselves to be transformed by God, humbly at His service and abiding with His will.

At this moment in the Liturgy, we can hear in our hearts God's response to this ultimate offering of ourselves for His glory. By offering ourselves in service and as praise, He in turn praises us! We can hear Him say to us what he said to Zephaniah.

> The LORD, your God, is in your midst, a mighty savior, Who will rejoice over you with gladness, and renew you in his love, Who will sing joyfully because of you,
> as on festival days. I will remove disaster from among you, so that no one may recount your disgrace. At that time I will deal with all who oppress you; I will save the lame, and assemble the outcasts; I will give them praise and renown in every land where they were shamed. At that time I will bring you home, and at that time I will gather you; For I will give you renown and praise, among all the peoples of the earth, When I bring about your restoration before your very eyes, says the LORD. (Zephaniah 3:17-20)

We now enter into the Eucharistic prayer. This part of the Mass is reserved for the ministerial priest, as by his ordination to the priesthood, *persona Christi*, that is, in the person of Christ; having authority to offer this sacrifice of praise to God the Father, and to invoke the Holy Spirit who transforms the bread and wine into the Body and Blood of Jesus. During the Eucharistic prayers, the priest makes the offering on behalf of all creation, and the people respond throughout the prayers in words of praise. The high point of praise comes when the priest invites us to acclaim:

"Holy, Holy, Holy, Lord God of hosts. Heaven and earth are full of your glory. Hosanna in the highest. Blessed is he who comes in the name of the Lord, Hosanna in the highest."

The first part of this prayer echoes the words of the prophet Isaiah when he saw a vision of Heaven.

> "In the year King Uzziah died, I saw the Lord seated on a high and lofty throne, with the train of his garment filling the temple. Seraphim were stationed above; each of them had six wings: with two they covered their faces, with two they covered their feet, and with two they hovered. One cried out to the other: 'Holy, holy, holy is the LORD of hosts! All the earth is filled with his glory!'" (Isaiah 6:1-3)

Another vision of heaven is described by John in the Book of Revelation.

> At once I was caught up in spirit. A throne was there in heaven, and on the throne sat one whose appearance sparkled like jasper and carnelian. Around the throne was a halo as brilliant as an emerald. Surrounding the throne I saw twenty-four other thrones on

> which twenty-four elders sat, dressed in white garments and with gold crowns on their heads. From the throne came flashes of lightning, rumblings, and peals of thunder. Seven flaming torches burned in front of the throne, which are the seven spirits of God. In front of the throne was something that resembled a sea of glass like crystal. In the center and around the throne, there were four living creatures covered with eyes in front and in back. The first creature resembled a lion, the second was like a calf, the third had a face like that of a human being, and the fourth looked like an eagle in flight. The four living creatures, each of them with six wings, were covered with eyes inside and out. Day and night they do not stop exclaiming:
>
> "'Holy, holy, holy
>
> is the Lord God Almighty,'
>
> who was, and who is, and who is to come."
>
> (Revelation 4:2-8)

The second part of the Sanctus comes from the chant of the people as Jesus made His triumphant entry into Jerusalem. Depicted in this scene are crowds of people praising and rejoicing for they see Jesus, who offers salvation, humbly riding a donkey into the city.

> They brought the ass and the colt and laid their cloaks over them, and he sat upon

> them. The very large crowd spread their cloaks on the road, while others cut branches from the trees and strewed them on the road. The crowds preceding him and those following kept crying out and saying:
>
> "Hosanna to the Son of David;
>
> blessed is he who comes in the name of the Lord;
>
> hosanna in the highest."
>
> (Matthew 21:7-9)

This Scripture recalls an event that has painted for me a modern-day depiction of Jesus' triumphant entry into Jerusalem. Once while at a conference in Brazil, I witnessed the people of God demonstrate the essence of those words, "Blessed is he who comes in the name of the Lord. Hosanna in the highest." A great crowd of Brazilians, much like the crowd in the Scripture, were anticipating Jesus to walk among them. There was to be a Eucharistic procession followed by a time of Adoration. As Jesus was brought among the people, the Brazilians were throwing their garments, shawls, scarves, jackets, whatever they had, to the floor in order for Jesus to be honored as He was brought through the assembly. Many were moved to tears, some bowing heads as Jesus passed by, some keeping their eyes ever so focused on Jesus, and some were reaching out toward the monstrance as if to "touch the hem of his garment" (Matthew 8:34) in order to be transformed by His power as did the woman with the issue of blood in Scripture. They were acclaiming Jesus as Lord in a very demonstrative and reverent way. His holy presence moved those under His gaze to leave behind any self-consciousness or pride. They were caught up in praise and worship of the Messiah just as in Jerusalem. This was extravagant praise!

A friend once shared with me a video clip of a Eucharistic procession in Africa that was very similar to the praise that we saw in Brazil. The procession was taking place outside on a dirt road. Colorful garments were placed on the ground long before Jesus ever entered the area. I was inspired when I saw this beautiful act of anticipation, welcome, and exuberant praise of the African people.

Our crying *Holy, Holy, Holy*, from the Old Testament Scripture to the New Testament Scripture of Matthew when Jesus enters Jerusalem, and which is repeated in the prophetic vision of John in Revelation is our heritage of praise; our present praise, and our future praise. No matter where we are, at Adoration, traveling, during our personal prayer time, while doing chores at home, or even at work, we are disposed to receive grace. We are even more disposed when we participate in the Sacrament of the Mass, joining with the angels, saints, and heavenly hosts to sing the prayer of praise to God. This great treasure of the Sanctus, woven into the Mass, offers an amazing opportunity for us to enter into praise over and over again drawing more deeply into the heart of who we are as a people of praise. Truly, we can agree, "Blessed are those who are called to the supper of the Lamb."

Chapter 9
The Upper Room of Praise

Saint Pope John Paul II acknowledged the renewal of the gift of charismatic praise in the Church. He encouraged this form of prayer with "…the singing, the words and the gestures. It is…how does one say it? I can say that it is a revolution of this living expression (of the faith). We say that the faith is a matter of the intelligence, and at times also of the heart, but this expressive dimension of the faith has been absent. This dimension of the faith was diminished…scarcely there. Now we can say that this movement is everywhere…"[22]

In silence, with voice, singing, gestures, or dancing our praise is meant to bring us to a point of communion with God. This is really the heart of the message of praise. We open ourselves to grace and a personal encounter with the Lord in an atmosphere of praise. God is continually doing something new in us. There are seasons in our lives when God sees fit to come to us in new and extraordinary ways.

My husband and I were invited to attend an international gathering of leaders of the Catholic Charismatic Renewal from around the world. This Prophetic Consultation was one of three events that is leading up to the Golden Jubilee of Catholic Charismatic Renewal in 2017. Sponsored by the International Catholic Charismatic Office in Rome, the event's goal was one I consider both brilliant and unique: we were there to listen to what the prophetic voice of the Holy Spirit would say to us as representatives of the Renewal. This was quite different from a conference. We had a somewhat flexible schedule and there were planned periods for listening and discerning.

This event was to take place mainly in Bethlehem. We had one free day of excursion to Jerusalem concluding with a whole group visit to the Upper Room. It was the perfect place for us to continue our journey of listening to the Holy Spirit. Something was stirring in me before I left for the trip, I couldn't put my thoughts around exactly what it was; but I can best describe it as anticipation and a new resolve for God. Somehow, I sensed I needed to be more available to be used by God for the Kingdom. Something was awakening in me in a real, deeper, and new way, and a yearning in my heart was building for something more. With all that being said, I debated whether or not I should go on this trip up until the week before travel. I struggled even in packing. I knew in my heart that I would be blessed to be among the five others from our area who were attending whom we consider friends. I was grateful for the opportunity to be among others from around the world who share the same gift and grace of the Holy Spirit. For many this opportunity would have been a no brainer; however, I was giving much brain-power to something I believe God had ordained.

Getting one hundred plus people through the streets of Jerusalem to the Upper Room who speak several different languages is no small feat. We were separated into groups by language. Each group had an interpreter to guide them to the destination. The Upper Room is guarded by an attendant and usually you are urged to see the place and move on. Time is an issue for visitors. No instruments or celebrations are to take place in this sacred space. Certainly, large groups are not encouraged, and it seemed personal reverence would be considered appropriate by those who guard this space. The leadership of the Prophetic Consultation event had no real way of knowing what exactly could or would be allowed. Our language group was one of the last to enter. When we did, there was no need for the headsets or interpretation. We put our headsets aside as we were caught up in a wave of praise rising up to heaven, and it was as if the fire of God was consuming us.

There we were—representatives of all different nations, priests, deacons, bishops, and lay people—praising God in the Spirit as one unified voice and it was here that I understood in a new way the miracle of Pentecost. As the Scripture says, "And they were all filled with the holy Spirit and began to speak in different tongues, as the Spirit enabled them to proclaim." (Acts 2:4) We were praising in the Spirit, the language of the Holy Spirit. On this occasion, specific interpretation was not necessary as our hearts were united in praise and we understood each other supernaturally. We had approximately one hour of praise and worship in the Upper Room! We were accompanied by the strumming of guitar, which was not normally allowed. We had an authentic prayer meeting complete with praise, worship, prophecy, and empowerment! This was a mighty move of God!

In this sacred space, filled with praise from every continent, including gestures of kneeling, clapping, and hands lifted, accompanied by lively singing and, at the same time, present a sense of holy awe that defines part of who I am today. If I could use one phrase to describe this experience, it would be: *Holy movement*. The Spirit was moving in the people; the people were moving in the Spirit. There was a visible reality of the invisible God expressed by the people in many different ways and each one was beautiful and reverent. While this description may seem like spontaneous chaos, there was an undeniable presence of God and His peace. There were periods of silence and the prophetic voice of the Spirit was among the people. Others who were not part of our group were entering and were experiencing something dramatic. Some dropped to their knees. Others looked bewildered but were drawn to stay and experience more.

This supernatural event marks time for me. This is where I realized that the Lord had been revealing to me the great mystery, secret, and powerful weapon of praise. Here in an atmosphere of praise, grace came to me. One of our friends attending had an inspiration from the Lord, a very simple word for me. I don't remember the exact wording but I sensed something of a new birth occurring in my heart. I felt as if I left the Upper Room with the zeal of John the Baptist. This is totally not my personality and it feels prideful to write this, but at the same time, it's a testimony to the fact that God can transform hearts and when hearts are changed, lives are changed. We can't plan a transformation. Only God can do that. We can choose to place ourselves in situations to encounter God, and even so, transformation is the work of the Holy Spirit.

I could not have planned what took place in the Upper Room on that day. It was a Kairos moment; a grace moment happening on Holy ground, where Mary and the disciples had gathered to pray for the Promise of the Father – the Holy Spirit. And He did come, in a new way. The Holy Spirit can come to us in a new way even if we never visit the Upper Room. God wants to break into our hearts in the power of the Holy Spirit to change us and to change the world for His initiatives. Our job: Praise!

Chapter 10
Intentional Praise

As we have discovered, praise is a multifaceted prayer. It's more than being thankful, more than mere singing, more than a mindset that God is worthy. Praise is an act of the will and expression of the heart. Just as we discovered the power of praise in the Old Testament, the Festal Shout preceded by the call of the horn, we find it fulfilled in the New Testament, the praise of Mary and her cousin, Elizabeth. Linking the Old and New Testaments is the Book of Psalms, where we especially witness the sound, look, and desire of praise in the heart of the Psalmist. The Catechism states that The Psalms "both sounds the call to prayer and sings the response to that call: Hallel-Yah ('Alleluia'), Praise the Lord!" (CCC 2589)

David was the master of accomplishing this statement in human form. In his orchestrating praise, he sounds the call, and he sang the response with all his might. So too, did Mary sound the call to praise when she greeted Elizabeth at the Visitation. She also sang the response in her *Magnificat*. Mary was the perfect personification of the Psalms. Her entire life was a demonstration of living praise!

What does this mean for you and me? In the times we are living, it is necessary once again to sound the trumpet and call the people to praise. It's time again to sing the Psalms in abandonment. Like Mary, we too should sound the call, and sing the response of praise. Our duty is to listen to the Holy Spirit who prompts us to know when to sound the call and sing the response.

You and I must praise God as if our battles are already won, because they are already won. We know how the story will end. We're just working out the details. Some of the Old Testament examples of praise took place at times of life or death. New Testament praise, which is our praise, is for the life that's been promised, so we praise with contrite hearts overshadowed by grace.

In each of us is a testimony. A story of how God moved in our lives. In each of us is a Psalm, a reason for crying out to God. I once read that all of the Psalms have not yet been written. I believe that. We all have a personal Psalm. I will conclude with mine:

A Psalm of Praise

My soul was created for you, my God,
And I will praise your name forever
My soul an intentional dwelling place
Ever welcoming the Holy Spirit

In my youth you let me find you
Your love experienced profoundly
My life preserved and guarded
You placed your shield about me

You led me into the desert
To trust and depend in abandonment
My abundant tears you cherished
You dried them in due time
My soul sings of the favor of my brokenness
You strengthened me in desperation
Your hand forever upon me
Consoling my broken heart

You have prepared newness of season
True gladness and rejoicing
A new beginning from all eternity
Received as gift and grace

A consecration of trust and love
Complete with Trinitarian character

You have set me free, my God
Free from my insecurities
Free to proclaim your goodness
To act on your behalf
And to participate in your power.

Forever will I sing a melodious praise
I will lift my hands in surrender
For I have tasted of your favor
And my praise will never cease
For eternity is my desire

Only you can quench my thirst, O Lord
I drink deeply, O Love and Mercy
Forever will I sing a melodious praise
Eyes and heart looking up forever

May my lips and actions honor your name
Bringing others into the realm of your glory
The blasting horn to sound the call
A mighty hymn of praise

A never ending melodious song
On the lips of all your people
Hearts of stone
Now made flesh
To pour out praise before the King

Lavishly we praise with hearts made whole and new
Praise rising up into the heavens
Reaching the Throne Room of Grace
A new song of praise growing in intensity
To announce the King of Glory
Alleluia!

References

[1] "Meeting with the Young People of New Orleans-Address of His Holiness John Paul II." *Vatican.va*. Libreria Editrice Vaticana, 12 September 1987. Web. 1 December 2016.

[2] Ibid.

[3] Ibid.

[4] Ibid.

[5] Ibid.

[6] Ibid.

[7] Ibid.

[8] Ibid.

[9] Ibid.

[10] Ibid.

[11] St. Augustine, *Confessions* 1,1,1:PL 32,659-661.

[12] "The Prayer of Praise by Pope Francis." *Vatican.va*. Libreria Editrice Vaticana, 31 January 2014. Web. 1 December 2016.

[13] Ibid.

[14] "General Audience of Pope Saint John Paul II." *Vatican.va*. Libreria Editrice Vaticana, 10 July 2002. Web. 1 December 2016.

[15] "General Audience of Pope Saint John Paul II." *Vatican.va.* Libreria Editrice Vaticana, 26 February 2003. Web. 1 December 2016.

[16] "The Psalms: Voice of the Church and Medicine for Hearts: Commentary on Psalm 1, by Basil the Great." *RC.net.* Washtenaw Covenant Community. Web. 1 December 2016.

[17] "Psalms: Music of Heaven – Ambrose." *Crossroadsinitiative.com.* Crossroads Initiative. Web. 1 December 2016.

[18] "Sing to the Lord a New Song! – Augustine." *Crossroadsinitiative.com.* Crossroads Initiative. Web. 1 December 2016.

[19] Ibid.

[20] "Pope Francis: Long Faces Cannot Proclaim Jesus" *Radiovaticana.va.* Vatican Radio, 31 May 2013. Web. 1 December 2016.

[21] Ibid.

[22] "Private audience of Pope John Paul II with the ICCRO Council", Rome, 11 December 1979.

ABOUT THE AUTHOR

In 2013, Andi had the privilege to attend the International Prophetic Consultation gathering of leaders in the Renewal in the city of bread (Bethlehem, Israel), where she had a profound experience as she prayed in the Upper Room with leaders from all over the world for a fresh outpouring of the Holy Spirit. As a result of Andi's Upper Room experience she has answered the call to share with others the gift of the baptism in the Holy Spirit.

Although Andi's first ministry is to her family, she has a true gift of hospitality to those she meets through ministry. She and her husband often welcome international clergy into their home for refreshment and fellowship with the wider Body of Christ. This true love for caring for others and her desire to share her love of the Lord has led Andi to speak at many local events throughout Louisiana. Andi led her first international retreat in Nova Scotia, Canada in April 2016.

Some of Andi's local events include: the Southern Regional Charismatic Conference in Metairie, the Women's Regional Retreat in Lafayette, and the Women's Day of Refreshment. In addition, Andi has been part of a team that presents Life in the Spirit seminars for Seminarians at Notre Dame Seminary in New Orleans, Louisiana.

Andi's love of Scripture and her enthusiasm to learn about the things of God motivate her to continue to grow in her own faith journey. She is an avid reader and enjoys spending time with her family. Andi is a teacher by training with a Bachelor's Degree in Elementary Education and a Master's Degree in Administration and Supervision in the education field.

To learn more about Andi, please visit her webpage at: www.AndiOney.com.

Made in the USA
Columbia, SC
29 August 2024

40686958R00070